SO, YOU WANT TO BE A PHYSICIAN

Getting an Edge in the
Pursuit of Becoming a
Physician or Other
Medical Professional

EDWARD M. GOLDBERG

CONTENTS

ACKNOWLEDGMENTS

First and foremost, I would like to thank my wife, Linda Trytek,
for her continuous love and unwavering support in spite of
very long work hours and the challenges of living with me.

I would also like to thank Elvira Krug, my prior assistant, for typing
and retyping the initial draft of this book and enduring the challenges
of working with me. My thanks also go to Angela Houghton, my
research assistant, who has been invaluable in helping organize the
initial and updated book, follow up on student stories, and coordinate
the placement of the first and updated edition as an editor and
publisher. I appreciate the assistance of my high-school friend, Frank
Shuftan, in serving as an initial editor of the first edition of the book.

Finally, I would like to recognize all of the students
who have contributed to each edition and with whom
I have worked, some of whose academic brilliance and
research achievements have been exceptional. I, and their
patients, look forward to great things from them.

PROLOGUE

I have been a hospital administrator for thirty-eight years, and unlike many other hospital administrators, I've been known for being "physician friendly." In that time, I have made close connections with thousands of physicians representing all subspecialties. Each day, I have been acutely aware of the joys and tribulations physicians encounter in practicing medicine.

I went to Northern Illinois University, where I received a bachelor of science in marketing and graduated cum laude. Then I received a master of science in hospital and health services administration from The Ohio State University.

So how did I come to write a book on how to get into medical school?

Approximately twelve years ago, a member of my medical staff informed me that I had to get his son into medical school—or else. I explained to the physician that I had never really taken a full science course my entire life. I literally had to walk out of high-school biology my first day because I couldn't stand to see the pinned, dead, stinking frogs, and the smell of formaldehyde made me want to vomit. I made an agreement with the teacher that I would write a paper on mitosis and meiosis rather than attend the lab. I lasted only one day in high-school chemistry: when, on the first day of the school year, the teacher gave us homework, I said, "That's it for me—you're not supposed to give homework the first day of class."

So how could I possibly help an individual get into medical school? The doctor's response was, "You're a smart guy—you'll figure it out."

I asked our hospital's legal counsel if this would be an acceptable service to perform from a Safe Harbor / Stark II perspective, and she indicated that if I offered the service to all employees and physicians, I could offer my tutoring services without legal risk. Safe Harbor / Stark II laws prohibit the provision of payment in cash or gifts in kind to induce a physician or other health-care provider to refer patients to a hospital or other health-care provider. I have never turned anybody down who asked for this service, and until writing this book, I never charged for it. I have not only provided this service to children of employees and to members of the medical staff but also to individuals who have called me up and stated they know so-and-so, or are friends with so-and-so, or heard that I could perform this service. I asked only that they write to me after their interview and inform me if my coaching helped or not and then provide me with the questions they were asked so that I could pass them on to others. I utilized this input to write this book and as the foundation for my coaching services, for which I now charge.

My first student was just starting his sophomore year in college and attended an undergraduate program that had an affiliation with a medical school that would enroll two students each year in a guaranteed medical-school program. This was a unique program where neither he nor I would have to worry about his MCAT scores. Given that I couldn't change his grade point average or activities, all I could really have an impact on was his personal statement and his interview abilities. He had good grades, was an Eagle Scout, and had done community service—and had gone on a mission trip to Peru—so I had a lot to work with.

I thought of several possible interview questions, which I still utilize today. The individual was successful, and seven years later I helped him prepare for an interview for an ENT residency position, which he received. I have since tutored scores of individuals, not only for traditional medical-school programs but also six-to-eight-year medical-school programs, dental school, veterinary school, medical-school residencies, physician-assistant programs, and nurse-practitioner programs. I have an impressive success rate. I recognize that many of the individuals who have come to me have had good grade point averages and good or great MCAT scores. Many have had solid health-care activities, research, or service. But all my students have confirmed that I made a significant positive impact on their personal statements and their interview abilities.

It's ironic that an individual who never took science courses is teaching people to prepare for their residencies and assisting them on their path to becoming a physician, dentist, veterinarian, physician assistant, or nurse practitioner, although I have had significant exposure to physicians in thirty-eight years as a hands-on, physician- and employee-friendly hospital administrator.

What began as a service and an interesting hobby has evolved into this book and a passionate new profession.

Finally, it's important to point out that the observations that follow throughout this book—such as the differences between male and female candidates—are based purely on my personal experiences and are not meant to reflect universal statements.

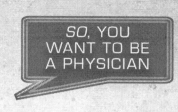

CHAPTER 1

WHY WOULD ANYONE WANT TO BE A PHYSICIAN?

I talk to numerous physicians every day. Many have told me that they are frustrated with medicine and have told their children not to try to become a physician. There is no question that these are very difficult times for physicians. They are being told what to do by the government, they are being told what to do by insurance and managed-care companies, and they are being told what to do by hospitals. Physicians are increasingly losing their independence, and being independent is one of the major reasons why individuals choose to become physicians. They are not only competing with other physicians but with physician assistants and nurse practitioners in drug and grocery stores and with hospitals. Reimbursements are declining, and physicians experience the same increasing pressures on their costs (i.e., malpractice insurance, technology, and hiring and maintaining employees) that all businesses encounter.

I often say, when the food on the table shrinks, table manners deteriorate. Right now, in health care, the food on the table is shrinking, and table manners are deteriorating. Unfortunately, things are likely to become worse.

Although I often bemoaned the trials and tribulations that affected me as a hospital administrator, I would probably rather be a hospital administrator than a pediatrician who is paged almost every night he or she is on call, primarily to respond to children's earaches. Likewise, an obstetrician who might have to risk a malpractice lawsuit on every case he or she performs. Obstetricians might have to remain in the hospital for up to thirty-six hours or more for a delivery, and then may only receive $900. That fee usually includes the eight to twelve prenatal visits as well. With some malpractice carriers not wanting to insure physicians who have had three or more claims in the last ten years, even if the physician was found innocent, it's a career with challenges and stress on top of having someone's life in your hands.

On the other hand, there are many medical and surgical specialties where individual physicians can make an extremely handsome living, enjoy the respect and admiration of their patients and community, and remain very happy with their careers.

Physicians do have the choice of becoming an employee of a hospital, or of a larger physician group, without having to be distracted by the tasks of operating a business. There would be no need to be concerned with hiring staff, performing billing functions, or enrolling in insurance and managed-care plans. Alternatively, physicians still have the opportunity to run their own practice and be independent. There is also the satisfaction of helping people when they are most vulnerable.

Interestingly, most dentists, veterinarians, nurse practitioners, physician assistants, and certified nurses that I have talked with are generally very happy with their career choice.

CHAPTER 2

WHEN SHOULD YOU START THINKING ABOUT BECOMING A PHYSICIAN?

I often tell students that it is never too early to think about becoming a physician. By giving this career consideration early on, you can shape your academic classes and experiences to help you achieve your goal.

Many of the students who come to me have known they wanted to be a physician since elementary school.

This can affect the courses you take. For example, take as many science classes as possible. Advanced Placement science classes are even better. Also helpful as you pursue this goal is providing service in the health-care world, perhaps by volunteering for a medical mission or being a scribe in the ER.

But the gold standard is working in a research lab—even if it's doing what may appear to be a menial task. If the opportunity presents itself, don't miss out, and if the opportunity doesn't present itself, seek out that opportunity.

CHAPTER 3

THINK OF GETTING INTO MEDICAL SCHOOL LIKE STAYING IN A HOTEL

n the 2013 edition of this book, there were 159 medical schools in the United States (133 MD and 26 DO), 54 in Mexico, and 59 in the Caribbean. In 2016, the Association of American Medical Colleges stated that there are now 145 accredited medical schools in the United States and 17 accredited schools in Canada. As of 2011, there were 60 medical schools in the Caribbean, although not all of the Caribbean schools are accredited. Only seven Caribbean medical schools have been accredited by the Accreditation Commission on Colleges of Medicine.

As stated in the 2013 edition of this book, there were 39,108 medical school applicants in the United States in 2006, of which 21,000 were rejected and only 18,108 accepted. In 2011 there were 43,919 medical-school applications, of which 24,689 were rejected and only 19,230 accepted.

In 2015, there were 52,550 applicants, 31,919 of whom were rejected and only 20,631 accepted into medical school. Over the past ten years, the numbers of applicants to medical school each year has steadily increased, from 39,108 applicants in 2006 to 53,042 applicants in 2016.

One prospective medical student was told, by what I consider to be a lower tier medical school in the Midwest, that they have 12,000 applicants for 200 spots.

The number of students accepted into medical school has gradually increased, but not at the same rate as the rise in numbers of applicants. As a result, the competition for acceptance into medical school has risen exponentially over the past decade.

In the 2013 edition of this book, applicants for medical school averaged 28 points of a possible 45 on the MCAT. Individuals who ultimately became medical-school students averaged 32 points.

The grade point average of accepted students was 3.5 to 3.8. The statistic on grade point average has increased slightly in 2016, and applicants are now scoring an average of 3.7 and higher. In addition, the average matriculant had an average GPA of 3.64 in the sciences. The MCAT was changed in 2015, and so those numbers are now different. These changes are discussed further in chapter 4; however, the MCAT scores for applicants to medical school now average 501.8 points of a possible 528. Individuals who ultimately become medical-school students have an average score of 508.7 points. [1]

In 2013, I suggested students aim for an MCAT score of 32 or higher to ensure that they have a good chance of acceptance into medical school. From my experience with the students I have coached in 2016, I have seen evidence of a much more stringent level of competition. Considering the increasing numbers of applicants, and changes in the MCAT scoring, I would suggest students aim to score 515 or higher on the MCAT, or in the ninety-third to ninety-fourth percentile or above, to assure they are in a stronger position in the application process.

I have seen students who fell below the criteria above who felt that they could compensate for this by having pages of non-healthcare extracurricular activities, including being involved in various sports (sometimes as team captain), playing musical instruments, dance, chess, violin, volleyball, karate, tennis and so on.

I don't want to break the students' hearts or their spirits, but I tell them that medical school should be considered like a hotel. The most important thing about a hotel is that it be clean and that there be a bed and clean sheets. You might go to the Ritz-Carlton, and they might have terry-cloth slippers and a bathrobe and chocolates, but if there is no bed, they don't meet the prerequisites for being a hotel. With that said, a good hotel needs good service, good cleaning, and perhaps even a good restaurant. Likewise, the two most important items to get into medical school are your grade point and MCAT score. Additionally, medical schools are now requiring service and healthcare experience as well.

I explain to students that if they took all the time they spent on their extracurricular activities and channeled it into studying to get better grades, taking a live, in-person Kaplan course, or receiving individual tutoring for a better MCAT score, and have some service and healthcare experience, they would be much better off.

Remember, the main components of getting into a medical school are your grades, MCAT score, and some service and healthcare experience. Without them you don't get to talk with me about improving your personal statement, your secondaries, or your interview abilities.

---

[1] Association of American Medical Colleges

In 2017, one of my students applied to a mid-tier medical school in the Midwest. The minimum qualifications to apply for this medical school included 150 hours of community service, 150 hours of healthcare exposure, and a general knowledge of the heathcare field. My prospective student was told that the students beginning in the 2016 school year had, on average, 862 total community service hours. In addition, these students also had an average of 1648 hours of healthcare exposure. The same medical school stated that they place an emphasis on research experience, academic accomplishments, and demonstrated leadership.

When medical schools state that they value community service and healthcare exposure, they want to see you involved in meaningful roles that demonstrate your interest in leading and helping others within, ideally, a healthcare related setting. Research is always a plus because it demonstrates an intellectual pursuit and the desire to learn. Being a scribe in the ER is a great experience, and shadowing a number of physicians is also a good experience.

My suggestion is to concentrate on your healthcare exposure and service hours, grades and MCAT score, which will get you the interview, and then work on providing the best personal statement, secondaries and interview possible.

I am now advising many of my college students that they should take a gap year, and I am recommending this for many reasons:

1. I believe it is too much pressure on almost anyone to be studying to get a 4.0 grade point average and at the same time taking a live, in-person Kaplan preparation course in their junior year of college.
2. If students do take Kaplan in their junior year, they are certain to be lacking some science or other MCAT-related course or courses that they would have taken in their senior year that would have helped them achieve a better score on the MCAT. By taking a gap year, I am recommending that as soon as they graduate from college, they immediately enroll in the live, in-person Kaplan or Prentice MCAT preparation course (not the Internet course) and then take the MCAT as soon as possible after the course. This allows students to have the best chance of concentrating solely on their grades as undergraduates.
3. It allows them to concentrate fully on studying for the MCAT in a live, in-person MCAT class (not an Internet course) after graduation.
4. It also allows students time to complete their applications for the next year and take the time to shadow physicians, perform research, be a scribe, or perform other service and exposure to healthcare activities that would help them attain the service and healthcare hours needed to be a successful medical school

applicant. Some of them could be performed during college, i.e., summers if they do not negatively impact the student's GPA.

I know this isn't the way that your grandfather did it. It's not the way your father did it. It's not the way your older brother and sister did it. It's not the way your college counselor may recommend. It's not the way your parents may recommend to save the most money, but I believe it's the most effective way to become a physician. Given the current high levels of competition, the time this takes is minimal considering the long career ahead. The improvement to your grades and your MCAT score, in addition to gaining the additional service and exposure hours needed, will increase your probability of being a physician.

I am willing to work with students who come to me under different circumstances, but this is a path that I often recommend when consulting with sophomores or juniors.

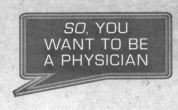

CHAPTER 4

HOW TO PREPARE FOR BECOMING A PHYSICIAN

My advice is to get the highest grades you possibly can, particularly in science. In 2015, the MCAT was updated. The exam now includes the following sections: "Chemical and Physical Foundations of Biological Systems," "Critical Analysis and Reasoning Skills," "Biological and Biochemical Foundations of Living Systems," and "Psychological, Social, and Biological Foundations of Behavior."[2] In addition to taking the MCAT, having an undergraduate degree in biology or chemistry is desirable. If you are offered the opportunity to take an anatomy course, take it.

For those applying to medical-school programs directly from high school, it is crucial to score as high as you can on the ACT. I have found an uncanny direct relationship between the ACT score and the MCAT score. Typically, a student receives a similar percentage ranking in the MCAT as he or she did on the ACT.

I highly recommend that students take the live, in-person Kaplan or other formal course for both the ACT and the MCAT. I also strongly encourage individual tutoring in addition to the Kaplan courses. I have found that the live, in-person Kaplan course usually increases the score in both the ACT and the MCAT significantly, and I have seen similar improvement via individual tutoring. Two to four points can easily make the difference in being accepted or not. Although the majority of the students I have talked to said, "Oh, I read a guidebook on my own," or "I took an online course," I recommend more formal guidance, as indicated above.

Additionally, for those who are thinking long-term and want to go to college and not a direct-from-high-school-to-medical-school program, my advice is to get into the best school you can.

---

[2] Association of American Medical Colleges

There can be exceptions, however. I know one physician, now a well-regarded subspecialist, who went to a well-respected university for his undergraduate program and only achieved a 3.6 grade point average. Even with a respectable score of twenty-nine on the MCAT, he ended up going to a Caribbean medical school. He felt going to a higher-quality undergraduate program actually hurt him.

In regard to your GPA, it's hard to judge whether it is more beneficial to participate in a demanding undergraduate program or one that may be less rigorous, as much of it can be the luck of the draw—that is, depending on which teachers and what classes an individual participates in. However, at the end of the day, a higher grade point average from a less prestigious school would probably trump a lower grade point average from a better school, within reason—that is, a delta of at least 0.3 or 0.4. Obviously, the best scenario is to have a great grade point average from a great school, so I'll stick with my original advice. Go to the best school you can get into, get the highest grade point average you can, and try for an even higher average in the sciences than your overall grade point average.

CHAPTER 5

SIX-TO-EIGHT-YEAR MEDICAL SCHOOL PROGRAMS

Approximately 15 percent of the students whom I have coached have applied for six-to-eight-year medical school programs. Some parents of students feel that the students might not be mature enough for a six-to-eight-year program, but my general feeling is that a bird in the hand is worth two in the bush. If an individual can be accepted to a six-to-eight-year medical school program, take it.

However, all of the six-to-eight-year programs that I am aware of have a minimum grade point average that must be maintained or you risk being disenrolled from the program. You may still go to that college, but you will no longer be in the six-to-eight-year guaranteed program. In some schools, the expected grade point average can be as low as 3.5, but it is typically a 3.65 or 3.75.

I worked with one student who did not maintain the required average and was dropped from the program. The student still had the opportunity to make a recovery by getting good grades and taking the MCAT for medical school, but for me it's kind of like the Woody Allen movie *Annie Hall*, where he suggested they kiss at the beginning of the date so they could get the tension over with. I feel the same way about the six-to-eight-year programs. If you can get in—why not?

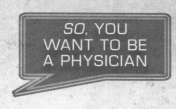

CHAPTER 6

BEST PRE-MEDICAL SCHOOL ACTIVITIES

As previously mentioned, some medical schools are now requiring applicants to have community service and healthcare experience. Medical schools are looking for well-rounded applicants, and real world experience enhances the ability of future doctors to work with patients of various needs and backgrounds. These activities may no longer be optional, and though it is important for the student to be interested and dedicated to the service and healthcare work they choose, careful consideration should also be given to organizations and facilities that will most likely give the student an edge in the application process. Taking on leadership responsibilities within a volunteer, service or healthcare role will further strengthen the student's application. I do not mean by this that managing a volleyball or softball team is relevant, and that is why I said service or healthcare experiences. This reinforces why I am recommending a gap year.

Students should make sure they maintain a balance with respect to their studies and other responsibilities, but aiming for approximately 10 hours of volunteer work a month during the school semester or more than 30 hours a week in the summer, will ensure that you are building the necessary hours that are needed as a medical school applicant. In gaining healthcare and volunteer experience, students should expect to stick with the same organization for at least 6 months, or a particular physician for at least 24 hours, in order to demonstrate their ability to dedicate themselves to both healthcare and community service.

Although most parents feel that volunteering as a greeter in a hospital is a meaningful experience and will help their children get into medical school, I don't believe that this is valid anymore.

I believe the new gold standard for activities that will help applicants get into medical school is, first and foremost, research. Even if it's minimal, this experience can be impressive, particularly if the student is asked back for a second or third year by a professor or physician who is leading the research. If the student can articulate the research, it's a plus in both the personal statement and the interview. If the student can articulate the research passionately, it's a bigger plus.

The second most helpful experience is that of a scribe in the emergency department of a hospital or with a hospitalist or internal medicine physician. This is a relatively new field. Typically, these individuals are college graduates who are in the emergency room transcribing the physicians' orders. They get to see a wide range of medical and surgical experiences and can utilize this as an excellent knowledge base in the personal statement and during the interview process.

A medical mission trip is always helpful because it's not only impressive in the student's personal statement but also can be utilized in interviews. Medical mission trips demonstrate that the student has a passion for helping others. I have never had a medical-student encounter a problem by mentioning participation in a medical mission during an interview. During a medical mission, students perform functions that are appropriate (taking a history and physical, teaching patients about hygiene, taking weights and heights, etc.), and every student I have coached has indicated that this assisted in the interview process. More information on medical brigades can be found in Chapter 22.

Unfortunately, there was one student whose father was an oral surgeon, who came to me one year after he was not accepted to dental school. In the student's first discussion with me, the student told me he informed the interviewer that he personally performed extractions during a medical mission in Africa. I felt the student was trying to impress the dentist conducting the interview, but the American Dental Association bylaws indicated that no one should perform any function for which they were not licensed in America—even if they were in Africa. The student was turned down. Although I continue to believe that medical missions are important, I always advise students that they shouldn't do anything that they are not licensed to perform in America.

Although the hands-on experience and cultural understanding and sensitivity gained on a medical mission trip can be very impressive in the application and during the student's interview, the student should emphasize that their desire above all else is to serve others. Some medical school interviewers may use the student's international experience and as a way to quiz them about their knowledge of the healthcare needs in their own community. Students should be prepared with a solid response in order to show their knowledge of healthcare both abroad and at home.

Another way for students to demonstrate their commitment to the field of medicine is to get a certified nurse's aide certification or EMT certification. Students with these certifications may find more doors opening to them within healthcare, and as a result, gain relevant healthcare hours towards your medical school application.

Organizations and programs to consider for gaining relevant healthcare experience

1. Patient care in a hospital
2. Shadowing physicians
3. Nursing homes and assisted living facilities
4. Supervised homes for individuals with developmental disabilities
5. Medical mission trips
6. Medical clinics for patients without insurance or financial resources
7. Emergency Medical Technician (EMT) certification

Organizations and areas to consider for gaining community service hours

1. Big Brothers Big Sisters
2. Habitat for Humanity
3. Senior service organizations
4. Wellness programs for children
5. Homeless shelters and employment service centers
6. Youth centers
7. Muscular Dystrophy Association Summer Camp and similar programs
8. Literacy programs
9. Food banks
10. Programs benefiting those with hearing and vision impairments
11. Special Olympics
12. Soup kitchens
13. Medical / Dental Brigades

CHAPTER 7

CUTOFF DATES TO DROP A CLASS WITHOUT IT ADVERSELY AFFECTING YOU

From your very first class at college, and for every semester going forward, you should know what the cutoff dates are for dropping classes without it affecting your transcript or grade point average. If you know that the goal is to achieve a 4.0, and you discover that you did not achieve an A or at least a solid B+ on the very first exam, drop the class. You can always take it in the summer or in the next semester or year, and also there's no harm in graduating in five years. They're not going to look to see if you graduated in four or five years. They are going to look to see if you had a 4.0 or 3.9. So if you're not doing well in class, drop it.

C H A P T E R 8

GET YOUR MEDICAL SCHOOL APPLICATIONS IN EARLY

Many students are under what I believe is a misconception that they have from June until December to get their medical school applications and secondaries in because medical schools indicate that applications are open from June to December. I believe they are sorely misinformed. I have seen students with similar grades and MCAT scores accepted if they applied earlier but rejected if they applied later. The same is true with your secondary responses because your application is not complete until your secondaries are submitted. It is clear to me from coaching students for years that students with the same GPA and MCAT scores whose applications and secondaries are submitted earlier have an advantage. I know the schools will not admit that this is so, but I know it is.

CHAPTER 9

LETTERS OF RECOMMENDATION

The most important thing about letters of recommendation is *don't wait*. You should be thinking as early as your freshman year about getting letters of recommendation from your professors. It's important to make sure that you not only know the professors but that they know you well enough that they would feel comfortable writing a letter of recommendation to support your application. This means that you know them both in the classroom and out of the classroom during professor office hours and develop a relationship with them. Taking more than one class from professors, if possible, is a great way for them to get to know you better. You also need to participate in class and stay in touch with them after the year is over. Speak to them in person well in advance, ask if they have the time to write a letter of recommendation for you, and inquire as to whether or not they feel that they know you well enough to write a positive letter of recommendation for you. You need to make sure that your interactions with them are solid enough and positive enough that they will write you a very strong letter of recommendation. It isn't something that you should be thinking about at the last minute. This is something that you should be thinking about before your first class as you go through each year of college.

CHAPTER 10

THE PERSONAL STATEMENT

As I've mentioned, great grades, meaningful activities, and nailing the tests not only get your foot on the ladder but also put you a few steps ahead of the competition.

But that's mostly the quantitative side of things.

Now it's time to show quality in two areas of critical importance: the personal statement and the interview process. Here is where the careful reader, and serious medical-school candidate, will find value added.

I have advised my students and their parents repeatedly that they should show me their personal statement well before they turn it in so that I can make suggestions or possible revisions. Unfortunately, a high percentage of students send me their personal statements the day before it is due or after they've already sent it in to their schools of choice. I usually respond, "What do you expect me to do? We can't change it because it's too late." Or I try to expedite a one-day exchange of suggestions. Some students and their parents will call me the day before their interview, even after I have explained and stressed repeatedly that it is a multiweek process.

I believe the personal statement usually needs to tell a story in a very distinct fashion. Many schools might say, "Describe a challenge that has changed your life," or "Describe a challenge that you have overcome." I have found that many students have something they want to include in their statement, often experiences or activities they are proud of; for example, an individual applying to dental school stated she was the president of the Premed Club. I advised her not to include that in her personal statement because it would look to the dental school as if she were second fiddle. But, no, the student spent time doing it, she was proud of it, and by goodness she was going to put it in there.

So, the most important thing is that the student carefully reviews what it is the schools are asking—and then respond to what they're asking, rather than just say what the student might want to say. I know this can be hard.

Assuming that the personal statement allows you to say whatever you want and does not have specific instructions, the student can choose to highlight good grades, his or her MCAT score, research experience, a mission trip, or health-care experience. I prefer to stick to a pretty normal path, starting with an interest and achievement in the sciences and then discussing overall grades if they are positive. If the science grades are better than the overall grades, mention it. If not, do not lie; simply mention what your science grade point average is. If your overall GPA is better than your science GPA, which would be unfortunate, simply stress your overall GPA.

Typically, I like to see some type of unique experience, such as valedictorian, salutatorian, Eagle Scout, leader in a group, research assistant, or any meaningful project or mission to help the community or humanity. Finally, the student should demonstrate commitment to helping others. If you have the grades, the ACT or MCAT, and some unique personal service or mission, I would go with that.

Many students think they need to be cute or unique or differentiate themselves by providing responses that are too extreme. If you don't have an ideal GPA or MCAT score, then you may need to explain the deficiency. Perhaps there is a legitimate explanation, which would be great, but be careful. Explanations that may involve drinking before the test, ADD, or breaking up with your boyfriend could just get you in more trouble. However, unfortunate legitimate explanations such as contracting mono or having a family member die could help explain a deficiency appropriately. But if you have demonstrable excellence in these areas, I recommend sticking to the basics.

CHAPTER 11

THE INTERVIEW PROCESS: THE GOLDBERG METHOD[3]

First, I'm like Sherlock Holmes or a journalist interviewing the student and trying to pull out every bit of information the student has—grades, coursework, ACT, MCAT scores, community service, volunteering, mission trips, Boy Scouts, Girl Scouts, research, sports, hobbies, and interests. Everything, including the kitchen sink.

If Art Linkletter were still alive, I could send him some of the things my students have said to me in the very first session that would surpass the statements made by kids from the show *Kids Say the Darnedest Things*. I could also send them to Ripley, but he wouldn't believe it.

Now, I understand that because it's a very informal discussion and I'm not "threatening," students may say things to me that they might not say in front of a physician from a medical-school admissions committee. Although most statements are appropriate, I have had students tell me the following reasons when I first ask them why they want to be a physician:

- "I think it would be great to get girls."
- "I think it would be a lot of fun."
- "My mom wants me to be a physician."
- "My dad wants me to be a physician."
- "My grandfather wants me to be a physician."
- "I could make a lot of money."
- "I think it would be the right profession for me."
- And the all-too-familiar "I want to help people."

---

[3] Please refer to chapter 17, "Receiving Your Desired Residency," to find more information on The Goldberg Method.

I wish I were joking, but I'm not. It's at this stage in the game that I explain to the students that their desired medical school was not founded in 1859 so that 150 years later they could have fun or make a lot of money by being a physician. I explain that they have to sell themselves to the school and explain what they can contribute to their patients, the school, the other students, humanity, and the field of medicine.

Then I become a playwright. The student writes the script, and I make recommendations. Our goal is to provide distinct responses to at least three and possibly four questions, each of which should be no more than one paragraph and each of which needs to be memorized exactly as we write them.

The Goldberg Method encourages the use a conversational, not formal, writing style during the interview preparation phase. Students will write responses to the following three questions, and each answer should be nine to twelve sentences in length, as the responses will need to be memorized:

1. **Tell me about yourself.**

   This answer should reveal something about your personality including but not limited to your love of science and wanting to help people. There might be some redundancy with the answer to the question "Why do you want to be a physician?" You can begin to talk about how you enjoy science, how you won a science fair, how you enjoy helping the homeless, and the beginnings of your love for science and helping people. This answer should end with something about your personality, such as your hobbies and your interests (e.g., "I love to play piano and play soccer").

2. **Why do you want to be a physician?**

   This one should be a little more in-depth and should talk about shadowing physicians; more advanced levels of science, such as research, anatomy, biochemistry, physiology, and so on; and the deeper rewards you receive from helping others (e.g., on medical brigades or other service trips) or that perhaps your parents who are physicians have received from helping others. There may be some overlap with the "Tell me about yourself" question. This should end with some type of indication that you wish to help patients one at a time or that it's about the patient, not you.

3. Why do you want to go (here)?

This will take significant research either online or using written material distributed by the individual medical school you wish to go to. One of the best ways that you can receive direct information is from students who have gone to or are currently going to that medical school, and in this case, with their permission, you should mention them by name. For example, I might say that Susan Jones, a third-year medical student, has informed me "how wonderful the faculty are" or "how noncompetitive the medical school is" or "that the faculty are willing to work with students one-on-one" or "how easy the medical school makes it to learn." Such personal references make for an excellent explanation of why the student would want to go to that medical school.

I believe that, in most business interviews, interviewers ask themselves if the interviewee is someone they would want to work with. I believe that internally this decision is made very rapidly. I think it's the same for medical-school interviews. That's the reason I place so much emphasis on really getting down the answers to three questions instead of hundreds of questions. I believe one of these questions is usually asked at the beginning of the interview, and once the tone is set in a positive fashion, I think the game is usually won.

What I really want the students to do is have the individual who is interviewing them end up rooting for them. I can see it in my own interactions with the students who come to me. The ones I am rooting for are the ones for whom I will give extra-special effort, because I really want them to be accepted. It's an unbelievable feeling when they call me, even before they call their parents, to tell me that the interview went well or, later, that they were accepted to medical school. The bottom line: *the purpose of all interviews is for the interviewees to have the interviewers root for them.*

The responses to the first two questions, "Tell me about yourself" and "Why do you want to be a physician?" can be drawn from the information provided in the initial practice interview.

The response to the third question, "Why this medical school?" needs to be researched specifically to match that medical school. In other words, the student needs to go online and find out what is unique about the medical school of interest and then follow up with the school after the interview, if possible. Some medical schools provide clinical experience in the first year; others make you wait. Professor-student ratio, what types of programs and research are performed, and other information should be reviewed so that students can sufficiently articulate why they want to go to this particular medical school. If students know someone in that medical school, they should seek him or her out and ask questions so they can reference this feedback (hopefully positive) in the interview.

Typically students will draft their responses, and because I interviewed them and know their total inventory of assets and attributes, I am able to guide them and ask why they left something out or put something in. Typically they e-mail this to me and I make suggestions, possibly additions or deletions, and we repeat the process until both the student and I are happy with the finished product.

There are occasions in which students and I do not agree, and I tell them it's their life and not mine, and I always defer to their judgment. But I try to explain to them why they should or shouldn't include a specific item.

After we reach agreement—or not—the students take the final product, whatever it is, and memorize it. Not only memorize it but "be it." Like Chevy Chase in the movie *Caddyshack* when he said, "You have to be the ball." You need to be the script. I then provide some general comments, and then I move from being like Sherlock Holmes / journalist / screenwriter to a nun with a ruler running through the script over and over.

One of my general rules is to not start a sentence with "well." For some reason, I have found this to occur almost ubiquitously among men and women of all cultures and nationalities.

The following are no-nos:

- Well...
- Ahh...
- Uhh...
- Umm...
- Well, actually...
- To tell you the truth...
- To be honest with you...

I explain to students that when they say, "Well, actually...To be honest with you...To tell you the truth," that actually means that everything they've said before that was a lie.

While we are going through the interview process, I literally keep a scorecard of the above no-nos, and after the students finish each rehearsal, I tell them how many times they said one until I hopefully "sensitize" the use of those words out of them.

After I believe they know the script *cold*, we work on the following:

1. Smoothness. Several of my students (mostly men) would look up in the air or shake their head as if they were reading the script in their mind. I tell these students that their responses need to come off naturally and smoothly, and if they bang their head or look up in the sky for the answer, it literally shows that they have memorized a script. Doing so blows the entire process.

2. Eye contact. I've learned an amazing thing from this process. Almost every woman seems to provide good, natural eye contact, and almost universally, males do not. Men look down, look away, look over your head, or look up at the ceiling. I need to work on men with this problem and sometimes have to say, "I'm over here." Why this is I'm not sure, but I assume it's because women are naturally concerned with others and most men just care about themselves.

3. What do you do with your hands and feet? Once again, most women seem to naturally know what to do with their hands. They keep them gently at their sides or in their lap but use them occasionally to make a point or show enthusiasm. Men, on the other hand, don't seem to be able to utilize their hands appropriately. Most of the time, the men's hands are like a robot's, stiff and at their sides, not moving during our entire discussion. On a rare occasion, their hands are waving up and down and are all over the place. Similar to a woman's use of her hands, the man's hands should be quietly at his side or on his lap but utilized occasionally to stress a point or express passion. Legs should be relatively still: no shaking up and down, changing positions only infrequently.

4. Posture. Probably 60 percent of the individuals I teach are women, and 40 percent are men. Almost every single woman, irrespective of culture or ethnicity, has had good posture. They sit upright toward the middle front of the chair, leaning slightly toward the interviewer; their body language says they are interested. Men, on the other hand, typically lean back lazily as though they are in their bedroom talking to some friends, or they sit up stiff like a robot. I explain to them that this will be the most important interview of their life and to demonstrate interest they need to sit toward the front middle of the chair, back erect, leaning slightly toward the person with whom they are talking. Sounds simple, but you would be amazed how difficult this can be for some men.

5. How you dress. Once again, the women seem for the most part to dress appropriately and on occasion come slightly overdressed. Almost every male student has

come in messy: 95 percent in gym shoes, 5 percent in flip-flops, typically wearing a shirt without a collar, and often with messy hair.

The only problem I have found with women is that approximately 20 percent have a nervous, inappropriate giggle or laugh. Unlike the men, where training has to be constant and hard, all I need to say to most women one time is, "Oh, so you're going to be a physician and tell Mrs. Jones her husband died and then giggle." After that, they typically take the criticism constructively, and the giggle does not occur again. Why women seem to be able to utilize feedback appropriately, but similar advice proves to be more difficult for men, I really don't understand. My wife says that culturally women are trained to respond to expectations and criticism more than men and that women, as child bearers, are hardwired to use eye contact to gain nonverbal information from others. I have no idea why, but there is a huge difference in interviewing ability between men and women.

6. Practice, practice, practice. I tell the students it's important to practice, not only alone, sometimes in the mirror, but with someone else to look at the script and go through it with them.

My philosophy is that although there are likely to be numerous questions asked during an interview, students should focus on just three main potential questions. Preparing for one or two more questions based on unique circumstances can also be appropriate. One of those questions might be, "Why did you wait one year after college to apply to medical school?"

7. The elephant in the room. If there is an obvious shortcoming or deficiency in your body of work—for example, you had a very poor GPA your first year but later made a recovery, or you had great grades and great research but blew the MCAT—I believe it is important to mention the elephant in the room. They've seen your scores and transcript, they know it, and they are probably too polite to ask about it, so you might as well address it. If there is a unique circumstance that's explainable, I say throw the Hail Mary and explain it.

I believe one of my most gratifying and meaningful coaching achievements involved a student who was a wonderful individual, attended a decent medical school, had a class rank near the middle of the pack, and had National Board scores of approximately 50 percent. This student really wanted to be a dermatologist. The student applied for the first residency match and did not match. Although she could have received an internal-medicine residency at a very decent program, she wanted to be a dermatologist—or not be a physician at all. I hadn't counseled this student yet but knew her father and saw them at our annual holiday party, and I offered my assistance. The student refused to accept my assistance. I tried to talk the student out of being a dermatologist, indicating that it is typically the top 1 percent of the class and 1 percent in the National Boards that are accepted to a dermatology residency, but this individual was determined to be a dermatologist.

After medical school this individual worked, without payment, for one year with a dermatologist who had an affiliation with a medical school. The individual assisted in writing an article for a dermatology journal and continued on to apply again for a dermatology residency. Again, no match.

The next year, this individual continued to refuse my offer of assistance. She worked on another article and a chapter of a dermatology book with a different person loosely affiliated with a teaching program. The individual then applied again for a dermatology residency and still did not match.

Now, the individual came to me and asked for assistance. In my long interview with the student, I asked if any of the interviewers asked about class rank or National Board scores. The individual indicated that the interviewers did not ask about either. I explained that, in my opinion, there was a bubble over the individual's head that the professors were looking at rather than the student. The bubble said, "I only received 50 percent in the National Boards and 50 percent in the class ranking." Why would they pick anyone who had those statistics when they could have individuals in the top 1 percent of each? I indicated that I felt the interviewee needed to address the elephant in the room and if the professors didn't bring it up, she would need to. The goal was to draw the attention of the interviewers to the person, her passion and achievements, and not her National Board scores.

When I asked the student why she wanted to be a dermatologist, she indicated that it was because dermatology made her feel like a well-rounded and total physician—finding the problem through observation, confirming it through pathology, and taking an action to correct it via surgery or medication. I have talked to many medical students who wanted to be dermatologists, and I felt that many of them wanted to be dermatologists because they were students who always wanted and achieved the best. They went to the best colleges, were first in their class, and went to the best medical schools because they were the best, and they wanted to be dermatologists because they were told that's the best specialty to be in. I knew other medical students who wanted to be dermatologists because of the high pay. Others desired the lifestyle, and some didn't want to be burdened by a pager, which almost all other specialties require.

This individual wanted to be a dermatologist because it made her feel like a total physician. The student had a passion and unquenchable desire. I suggested that she utilize the phrase "National Board scores don't take care of patients—physicians do." Then the interviewee could go on to explain that many individuals want to be dermatologists for the reasons mentioned above but this individual wanted to be a dermatologist because of her passion for the specialty. The student had already proven her passion through the articles and chapter that she had contributed and through her continuing efforts and determination to persevere in the specialty.

When I received a call from this student saying that she felt this final interview had gone much better than the prior ones, I started to cry, as I was really rooting for this individual to succeed. I felt she really deserved it. I would go to this person if she became a dermatologist. It was with equal tears that I received the individual's call to tell me that she had been accepted to a dermatology residency. I thought, good for this student and good for the program that was smart enough to see the true qualities of this physician above her board scores.

I had another individual who had a mediocre GPA at a mediocre college and a mediocre MCAT score. During my questioning, I spent over an hour with this individual trying to find if he had done anything unique. I repeatedly asked if he had done any research. To add to my disappointment, I felt the individual was generally unenthusiastic. I actually told the student I didn't think I could help him as there was no hook, like being an Eagle Scout or going on a medical mission. So after I told the individual that I didn't think there was anything I could do and was walking him to the door, I asked again, for what was now the fourth time, if there was anything unique or special in his background that could be utilized during an interview. Did he receive any awards, complete any research, or have a particular passion? Finally, he indicated that he had been working in a lab in southern Illinois on the weekends for the past two years.

I told the individual to have a seat again and tell me about what he did in the lab. He told me about his experience at the lab with an illumination, brightness, and enthusiasm that he hadn't displayed in the previous hour. He intricately explained his work placing probes on mice and performing EEGs under different scenarios.

It sounded to me like exciting, meaningful research, and the individual sounded excited and enthusiastic about it. I said, "Don't change one word, and describe this in your interview exactly as you just did to me with the same level of enthusiasm." I indicated that even if the interviewer introduced himself and then tried to end the interview, his description of the research needed to be told to his interviewer no matter what. This individual was accepted into medical school.

8. If they ask you if you have any questions, you should be prepared to ask something. Two suggestions are

   a. What made you want to become part of the faculty here?
   b. What about this program are you most proud of?

Great Answers to the Three Questions

1. Tell me about yourself

- I graduated from Boston University with a BA in psychology and biology. Throughout my life I have had passions for understanding the complex human body and helping those in need. Growing up in New York City with Spanish physicians as parents, I developed a great appreciation for the customs and traditions of different cultures. I speak both Spanish and English, and I became deeply fascinated with the human body. I consider myself a very social person, and I love to talk and interact with people. My love for interacting and my passions have led me to volunteer throughout my life, travel to Honduras on a global medical brigade, and tutor inner-city Chicago public high school students. Although I struggled freshman year in college, my perseverance and optimistic attitude allowed me to adapt new learning strategies to ultimately succeed.

- I am from Algonquin, Illinois, attended Jacobs High School, and graduated with a 3.9 GPA. While I was there, I was involved with the music program. I played the violin and even had the opportunity to be section leader and first chair of my high-school orchestra. I was also an executive board member in the music honor society, Tri-M, and acted in just about every play and musical offered at my high school. I was also very involved with the National Honor Society and performed service projects in the community and worked with every age, from elementary school to people in the nursing homes.

- I have always been interested in science and helping people. I appreciate the satisfaction I gain from helping others and the relationships I am able to develop. For six years I worked as a medical assistant and transportation manager for a medical practice. I enjoyed medical school and loved my clinical rotations. I work hard at everything I do. In my spare time, I play numerous sports, teach and learn dance, and participate in filmmaking.

- Growing up in Pepper Pike, Ohio, I became interested in science and medicine at a very early age. When I was in the second grade, my grandfather suffered a heart attack while I was alone with him on a fishing trip. After that terrifying accident, my grandparents explained the concept of heart disease. I then became fascinated with reading through the encyclopedia learning about science and the human body. Many years later, I entered college at the Ohio State with a zeal for knowledge and an interest in pursuing a career in medicine. There I excelled in a wide variety of science and liberal-arts courses, achieving a 4.0 GPA. I decided to major in Spanish in order to better understand the needs of a growing segment of the population. I also started volunteering as a tutor helping to bridge the achievement gap between Spanish-speaking students and their peers. Two and a half years ago, I began working twenty-four hours a week as an EMT with the Columbus Fire Department and board member of the Columbus Police Department First Responders. In my free time, I enjoy taking long bike rides and preparing healthy meals for my friends and family. I am a hardworking individual who understands the value of teamwork, and I am dedicated to treating my patients and peers with dignity.

- Science classes have always been my favorite, and this interest only increased with dissections, chemistry experiments, and laboratory demonstrations. At the University of Illinois, my passion for science led me to pursue experiences in the Health Sciences Scholars Program. I was a volunteer at the U of I Cardiovascular Center for three years. Interacting with and developing relationships with these patients was the highlight of my volunteering experience; however, I wanted to be able to help these patients more clinically. I joined an organization that allowed me to provide first aid for patrons of campus events, and I am currently training to become an EMT. My experience studying models of heterotopic ossification has motivated me to work as a research assistant in a wound-healing laboratory at U of I. Working in the scientific field, engaging in clinical environments, and delivering clinical care to patients has heightened my desire to become a physician.

- I have made my academics and education my priority. From a young age, I started taking on extracurricular activities to broaden my interests. I'm a very meticulous person, so I enjoy hobbies like sewing and clay sculpting. I have had the opportunity to be a part of the health-science community by volunteering and participating in community-outreach programs. I've always enjoyed the sciences from elementary-school science fairs to laboratory work. I also take every opportunity to meet new people and make lasting connections. Every medical experience I partake in and interaction with other medical professionals confirms my love for science and my desire to become a physician.

- I've wanted to be a dentist from a young age and have interned with Dr. S. and Dr. D. to further my interest in the dental field. Along with my studies, I have been involved in my service fraternity, Alpha Phi Omega. I've caroled for nursing homes, painted at a women's shelter, and volunteered at carnivals for kids with special needs. I am also a morale captain for Dance Marathon. In that position, I make trips to the University of Iowa Children's Hospital and encourage people to help raise money for the Dance Marathon event. I am an active member of the art group Artisans, which allows me to experience different forms of art. I've worked with fine art, glass, jewelry, paints, and even pottery. I am currently a senior attending Augustana College and am finishing my biology major and biochemistry minor.

  During my time at college, I have had the opportunity to have different research experiences with two different professors: Dr. G. on the topic of hominid tooth evolution and Dr. S. on the topic of oral microorganisms. These were both interesting topics, and I enjoyed having the opportunity to work one-on-one with these two professors. I also have three jobs on campus. I am a morning worker for the recreation center, an admissions ambassador that gives tours and calls prospective students, and an anatomy tutor.

- I attended Carl Sandburg High School, and my grade point average overall was 4.069 and my science average 4.125. I was actively involved on the tennis team. I played second doubles and qualified for state all four years. My freshman and sophomore years, we finished sixth in state, and my junior and senior years, we finished fourth in state. I've also volunteered for four years at Saint Alexius Medical Center in Hoffman Estates and was asked to apply for a position in the Radiology Department. I have very much enjoyed my time here at Saint Xavier, and my GPA is 3.95. I also am secretary of Kappa Gamma sorority. I am still an active leader on the tennis team and play the top spot for singles and doubles. I am also the public relations cochairman of the prehealth club and a member of Habitat for Humanity.

- I grew up in Highland Park, Illinois, and went to Highland Park High School. My mom works for a nonprofit art organization called Art Encounter, and my father is a physician. I graduated from the University of Pittsburgh in 2009 with a 3.5 GPA. My senior year I was active in research working for the Behavioral Medicine Research Group, where I trained participants to use devices that measure stress in real time. I'm an avid soccer player. I played all four years in high school and am still playing in leagues in the

Chicago area. In addition to soccer, I enjoy cooking and reading. I also recently started playing golf again after adjusting my horrendous swing.

- I grew up in Arlington Heights, Illinois, attended Buffalo Grove High School, and am now a senior at Duke University. I am a biology major with a chemistry minor and a certificate in global health. I have an overall GPA of 3.82 and a science GPA of 3.92, and I obtained a thirty-eight overall score on the MCAT. I have developed a passion for global health throughout my time at Duke and pursued this passion by writing and being awarded a grant to conduct research on childhood undernutrition in rural southwestern Kenya the summer before my junior year. I have ample leadership experience through the Duke organization Project WILD, where twice a year I have led crews of seven to ten inexperienced freshmen on a one- or two-week backpacking trip. This past summer I shadowed a pediatric infectious-disease specialist at John Stroger Hospital once a week. Lastly, I have also been involved in various other organizations through Duke University, from tutoring elementary children to working in a *Drosophila* lab.

- I am from Palatine and come from a family of doctors. My parents are both internists. For high school I went to Loyola Academy in Wilmette. It was far from my house, but I could not have asked for a better high-school experience. A unique aspect of my high school was the awesome service opportunities that were there. My favorite experience was traveling down to Cairo, Illinois, to fix up broken-down homes and stores. It was refreshing to see the citizens we worked with remain enthusiastic and optimistic despite living in a ravaged town.

I attended college at Georgetown and looked to provide service with a medical focus. I became a part of the Georgetown Emergency Response Medical Services. As a biochemistry major, I wanted to learn how the scientific process worked as part of a lab group. I joined Dr. T.'s analytical chemistry lab group to analyze molecular effects on fuel cells. I synthesized platinum polyoxometallae nanoparticles and analyzed their electrochemical properties to determine their stability and potential suitability for fuel cells. The American Chemical Society awarded me with the College Chemistry Achievement Award for my work inside and outside the classroom.

When I was not working in the lab or as an EMT, I worked as the director of purchasing at an on-campus grocery store. I coordinated orders with more than forty vendors on a weekly basis and was able to introduce some new health-related products to the Georgetown community. I graduated from Georgetown this past May and have been working as an emergency-room scribe for doctors.

- I was born and raised around Naperville, a suburb of Chicago. My mother is a pediatric anesthesiologist, and my father is a communications engineer. I am a senior at MIT, where I'm majoring in aerospace engineering with information technology and minoring in public policy. I am fundamentally a problem solver—I see a problem or a need, and I try to address it. From my Eagle project when I was a Boy Scout to my engineering major and my work as an EMT, I have always tried to fix things. In addition to this, I have a wide variety of interests. I really like learning about politics and history—hence my public-policy minor. I also enjoy sailing, scuba diving, hiking, and many other activities, but fundamentally, if I can make something better, if I see a need that I can address, if I see an improvement that can be made—I'll do it.

- I was born and raised in Hong Kong. I completed my undergraduate degree in biology with departmental honors from Lehigh University. I have devoted much time to research, initially at Lehigh pursuing cell biology in the gap-junction field and currently at the Chinese University of Hong Kong conducting orthopedic research. I speak several languages, including English, Mandarin, Cantonese, and German, and also spent two years in high school learning Japanese. I volunteered in health-related activities in Pennsylvania and Guatemala. I hope to one day combine my interest in foreign cultures and languages, research, and passion to help people through medicine.

- I grew up in Buffalo Grove, Illinois, and I am the son and nephew of two pediatricians, so I have been exposed to pediatrics my whole life. I received my undergraduate education at the University of Rochester, where I played baseball, majored in chemistry, and minored in Spanish. I currently attend Rush Medical College in Chicago and finished in the top third of my class, and I received a 222 on USMLE step 1 and a 248 on USMLE step 2 CK. Besides academics, I am most proud of the work that I have done at NLVS, which is a clinic in West Rogers Park in Chicago. The clinic is entirely student run, and it primarily serves the South Asian community. I've volunteered there once or twice a quarter since my M1 year. I was also the Rush treasurer for a year and raised more than $500 by organizing a medical-school basketball tournament. Besides medicine, I am obsessed with Chicago sports and have started running and biking. I recently completed two races called Muddy Buddies and the Urbanathlon. My ultimate goals are to finish a triathlon and a marathon.

- I am a triple major in biology, premedicine, and psychology at Augustana College, and I have always had interests in the sciences and in helping others. I intern for the Child Abuse Council and volunteer at a women's abuse shelter. I have learned the impact that one person can make, and similar to my experience on the crew team, I can see the impact that people working together can have. I have been blind in one eye since birth and am an asthmatic, which limited me athletically and socially as a child, so I devoted my childhood to learning and helping others. Above all, I want to be able to use my knowledge to help people.

2. Why do you want to be a physician?

- Growing up, family dinners were dominated by conversations regarding coagulation factors or the GI tract. My parents would quiz me days later, and I would strive to better understand what they were trying to teach me. Ever since, I have developed an immense fascination for science, especially for the human body, and have always wanted to keep learning. Also, when my family moved to Oak Park, Illinois, from Barcelona, our community helped my family find good schools, learn American traditions, and quickly make friends because my brother and I were lonely. These experiences instilled in me an unrelenting passion to give back to my community—just as my community helped me—and conduct research to better understand the beautifully complex human body.

- When I was in middle school, my friend's house caught on fire, and she was stuck inside. The paramedics sprang into action and were able to save her. The responsiveness and care they provided inspired me, and I realized I wanted to help people by becoming a physician. In school, I began to focus my course load on the sciences and noticed that I enjoyed each class I took. This year I am performing a research experiment at Colorado University of Boulder with Dr. Hoeffer at the Institute of Behavioral Genetics, and I find this very exciting and gratifying. When I began volunteering at Good Samaritan Medical Center, my desire to pursue medicine was strengthened.

- When my mother suffered a heart attack at the beginning of my second semester of college, her doctors addressed her unique issues with astounding empathy. I realized that decades of technological and clinical advancements were brought to bear in order to save her life. This challenging time reinforced my lifelong interest in science and medicine. I trained as an EMT in admiration of the responders who helped save my mother's life. Then I began working with the Columbus Fire Department, responding to a wide variety of emergency calls. Black or white, young or old, no matter what language they speak, we respond to people of all backgrounds, working as a medical team to provide high-quality care. Throughout my undergraduate career, I shadowed three different internists, a level-one trauma team, a general surgeon, a general cardiologist, and an electrophysiologist cardiologist. I watched as these doctors encouraged their patients to become active participants in their own health care and promoted health literacy among members of underserved communities. As a physician, I want to be a scientist, teacher, and advocate, continuously learning to better serve my patients' health-care needs.

- Being a doctor is, in my opinion, a noble and selfless profession. I want to dedicate all my efforts toward helping others in need, especially those who lack adequate health care. Over the years, I have accumulated life experiences through shadowing and volunteering in clinical settings that have only heightened my passion to pursue this profession. I have always enjoyed and excelled in biology and the life sciences. Part of the reason why I'm so engaged in research is because I'm fascinated with all facets of biology, including learning and physically performing different experimental techniques. This allows for a hands-on way of learning and critical thinking that would assist me in becoming a better physician. I would like to be a physician who works in the community helping people without access to care now and at the same time assisting in research that helps people in the future.

- My personal experiences as a volunteer, research assistant, and first-aid provider have been incredibly affirming, but it has been my experience observing the care of patients that has most significantly heightened my desire to become a physician. I am currently a volunteer at the Saint Alexius Medical Center Hospital Emergency Room. It is heartbreaking to watch a physician tell a spouse that her husband may not make it through the night. Majoring in biopsychology, I shared in the disappointment of the staff when a patient suffering from panic attacks refused to acknowledge the severity of his condition because he was feeling fine in the moment and didn't want to be admitted. These experiences have given me a profound respect for physicians who, in the face of these difficulties, strive to work through their frustration and enter the next patient's room with a new attitude and the same amount of sincerity. I want to be a physician to utilize my clinical and interpersonal knowledge to provide the best quality of care for my patients.

- I have always enjoyed science and excelled in it. I knew I wanted to be a physician after I became involved in several different facets of the profession. I shadowed physicians from internal medicine, infectious disease, and orthopedics, talked to medical-school faculty and students, volunteered at hospitals, and joined medical-exposure programs for students. Because I'm a person who enjoys building relationships, I was excited to see all the physicians I shadowed utilize not only their knowledge and skill but also their patient-physician relationships to improve their patient's treatment. The internist helped some of his patients' health by improving their diets and others by getting them to quit smoking, the infectious-disease physician continued to follow up every day with an insurance company to cover the medical costs of a patient who had been waiting years for treatment for his hepatitis C, and the orthopedic surgeon utilized his relationship with a football player to help him cope with his rehabilitation and retirement from football. Several months after his surgery, he came back to thank the surgeon for being able to walk even though he could no longer play football. It's the opportunity not only to apply science but to develop and utilize relationships that has heightened my desire to become a physician and to do the very best for every patient.

- I want to become a physician so that I can utilize my passion to help individuals improve their health. Everyone deserves a compassionate and motivated physician, and I have the potential to be one. I love learning about the human body, problem-solving, helping people, and challenging myself. Interacting with patients through volunteering and working as an emergency-room hospital scribe have reinforced my goal of becoming a physician. Working with emergency-room physicians has inspired me, and I want to have that same positive impact on my patients.

- I've wanted to be a physician for as long as I can remember. In grammar school I loved science classes and participating in the science fairs. I remember all of my science-fair projects, from paper-mache volcanoes to potato clocks. My mother is a pharmacist, my father is a physician, and my older brother just completed medical school at Rush and will be entering an ENT residency in Gainesville. Between high school and college, my family took a service trip to Peru and helped the poor and needy, and it made a significant impression on me regarding the positive impact that one person can make. I have seen the positive impact my parents have on others as health-care professionals and the great satisfaction that both of them receive in helping others. My desire to become a physician was heightened to an even greater extent when I volunteered at Saint Alexius Medical Center. I am committed to being a physician and helping others.

- My first interest in the profession came after I injured my knee playing soccer in college. I was treated by Dr. B. and his PA, Travis. Travis saw me for most of my preoperative and postoperative appointments. I was really impressed with Travis's care for me throughout my treatment, and I committed to learning more about the profession, as well as sports medicine. Although Travis piqued my interest in the profession, I was not absolutely sure the PA profession was right for me until after my shadowing experiences. I shadowed several PAs in orthopedics and dermatology, and they all said they felt their job was rewarding and stimulating. I liked how each PA I shadowed had a good rapport with the doctors, working well with them as part of a team but also working autonomously—in some cases seeing patients the whole day without the doctor on staff. I am also interested in the profession because the PA degree is so diverse. One PA I shadowed practiced in an emergency-room setting and was hired to work in orthopedics without having to retrain. Finally, I enjoy working with patients, and I liked the fact that the PAs

I shadowed were able to spend a little more time with the patients than other health-care members did.

- Medicine is at the intersection of everything I could want from a career. It involves working with people, lifelong learning, and the ability to help others. It also helps that I find the body, how it works, and how to manipulate it fascinating. My time in Kenya has made a huge impact on my life, and I have wanted to go back ever since I stepped onto the airplane in Nairobi. My dream is to spend time working with underserved populations, such as those in Kenya, and [insert medical school name] will give me the skills and tools I need to bring about a real change. I am aware of the dedication needed during the minimum of seven years until I can finally be a physician, and I relish the challenge.

- The biological sciences have always fascinated me. In fifth grade I gave a report on having a future career as a doctor, and I can vividly remember sharing my edible model of the eukaryotic cell with my seventh-grade class. My experiences and education as an undergraduate have fostered an intrigue for the practical applications of my studies. Medicine is a challenging career path, but it will allow me to help others and contribute to the community. It is special because the physician has the opportunity to relate to patients on a personal level and profoundly influence their lives. My grandpa was a physician who loved his work and was clearly moved by his encounters in medicine. After retiring at seventy-five, he still attended medical conferences with my mother and tried to keep up with medical news. As I get older, I hope to maintain the same passion for my work as my grandpa did for his. Medicine is a line of work where knowledge and procedural techniques are always changing. The dynamic atmosphere promises a job that will keep me on my toes while fulfilling a need to do something good for the community.

- I think medicine is a truly noble profession because of its focus on improving the lives of others. In addition, I think that being a doctor provides an opportunity for a varied and fulfilling professional life. A doctor can and sometimes must be a researcher, problem solver, businessperson, and leader in addition to a clinician, and I plan on embracing all of these roles fully.

- I've known from a very young age that I wanted to be a dentist because I've always had a fascination with teeth. Before one of my parents would have a dental appointment, I would actually put on my mom's dishwashing gloves and look in my parent's mouth and check for cavities. When I reached the eighth grade, I attended a career fair where a dentist gave a presentation on his occupation. I just remember feeling so excited when I heard about the different tasks of a dentist, such as working with your hands on a fine level and using that ability to help people. In high school I decided to further my interest in dentistry by interning with Dr. S. I became familiar with the tools and procedures, and Dr. S. even let me observe him on a regular basis, which was very exciting. It was such a great experience because I not only saw different procedures but also worked as a receptionist at his office.

Along with the internship, I was very involved with orchestra and continued my hobbies in making jewelry. I was even ambitious enough to make dollhouses. By playing the violin and working with art, I noticed my dexterity and attention to fine detail improved. Along with handwork, I have always loved helping people, so I decided to join the National Honor Society. I was a dedicated member and really enjoyed working in underserved areas. While attending college I had the opportunity to focus my interest on teeth through research with some of my college professors. My sophomore year I worked with Professor G. on the topic of hominid tooth evolution. Together we studied the structure of teeth to understand the evolutionary transition of the hominid species, and our research found that *Australopithecus africanus* is the closest genus to *Homo sapiens*. My passion to help others led me to a service fraternity called Alpha Phi Omega. In that group I plan activities to reach out to the needy. I have arranged caroling events and a senior-citizen prom at a nursing home, and I've even made hospital visits to the University of Iowa Children's Hospital.

- Having grown up the son of a pediatrician, the easy answer is that I want to do pediatrics because that's all I know. I am really comfortable working with children and their parents. Where some of my classmates are naturals in the OR, I am at my best when I'm telling toddlers jokes so they are not scared of the doctor, or explaining nutrition to a new mother. Also, I feel that in pediatrics you can positively affect your patients for the rest of their lives. The most frustrating thing about my medicine rotation was that the chronic illnesses were mostly caused by the parents' own behavior. Emphysema, obesity, and diabetes all could be prevented by modifying their behavior. As a pediatrician I want to be a role model and instill lifelong habits into my patients, like exercising, eating right, and not smoking, so that they won't develop these problems in the future. Plus, they are the cutest population, and there is nothing that puts a smile on my face more than a twelve-month-old yelling hello as soon as I walk into a room.

- Medicine interests me because I have always been fascinated by and excelled in science. I feel that I can better utilize my knowledge and my experiences—as an intern for the Child Abuse Council and as a volunteer with victims of domestic violence—to help others through this than any other career. I have been passionate about pursuing a medical career due to my interaction with physicians. As a child, I frequented doctor's offices due to my asthma and my blindness in one eye. I quickly noticed that the suggestions of these professionals led to great changes in my life and the betterment of my health. I knew that I, too, wanted to improve the health of others.

3. Why would you like to attend medical school here?

- SIU School of Medicine: I have always been able to adapt what I learned from past experiences to new challenges. SIU School of Medicine's focus on teamwork, problem-based learning, and serving the Illinois community perfectly complements what I wish to pursue in my life as a physician. I am especially interested in joining SIU's Psychiatry Interest Group and one of their many community-outreach programs. I believe SIU's innovative learning methods, friendly learning atmosphere, and emphasis on community service would mold me into both a leading scientist and compassionate physician.

- Medical College of Wisconsin: After my diverse clinical experiences at the University of Michigan–Ann Arbor and as a hospitalist scribe, I am eager to start clinical training in medical school, and I'm excited for the clinical apprenticeships during the first year. This program also establishes mentor relationships early on, which I found very valuable as an undergraduate. I appreciate the opportunity to pursue individual interests through the Scholarly Project. My interest in research and my strong self-discipline seem well aligned with this requirement. I would be honored to learn to treat patients one patient at a time at the Medical College of Wisconsin.

- Drexel University College of Medicine: The Program for Integrated Learning and Interdisciplinary Foundations of Medicine program are two outstanding programs. I am an interactive learner, so the PIL will allow me to learn more information and expose me to how physicians diagnose patients. I also work well with others, so this program will be beneficial because I will have to work collaboratively with other students to come to an agreement on diagnosis and treatment decisions. The IFM program is a positive opportunity for me because it has a traditional environment of academics while integrating interactive scenarios that I will need to collaborate on with other students in order to provide great patient care. I hope that I will be accepted and be able to contribute to the program at Drexel.

- University of Colorado School of Medicine: The University of Colorado School of Medicine BA/BS-MD program will allow me to develop the skills necessary to become a well-qualified and caring physician. The Summer Bridge program will provide a foundation necessary to succeed at the University of Colorado School of Medicine. The personalized scheduling program is a unique opportunity that I would appreciate participating in. Also, I collaborate well with other students, and this program will place me in an environment where I will work with others that have similar interests. I am hopeful that I will be accepted and be able to contribute to the program at the University of Colorado School of Medicine.

- Nova Southeastern University's College of Osteopathic Medicine: I strongly believe in Nova Southeastern University's College of Osteopathic Medicine's holistic approach to providing excellent medical care for patients. Nova's partnership with the Consortium for Excellence in Medical Education will allow me to pursue my desire of performing research and to find internship and residency opportunities with the school's support. I work better in intimate settings, and the small student-to-faculty ratio will allow me to work to my strength. I would join the Pre–Student Osteopathic Medical Association to surround myself with other students with similar interests, and I would join commu-nity-service organizations to help the surrounding community.

- Loyola University Chicago Stritch School of Medicine: Loyola's three-year Patient-Centered Health course ideally reflects the holistic health care that I greatly value. Through my clinical experiences at the University of Michigan–Ann Arbor and as a hospitalist scribe, I've learned how areas in a patient's life, such as social networks and resources accessibility, play significant roles in health outcomes and maintenance. Having taken five years of Spanish, I would like to be involved with the Spanish Medical Program, as I hope to provide the greatest level of care even when patients don't speak English as a first language.

- Northwestern University Feinberg School of Medicine: I am looking for a collaborative and noncompetitive learning environment, which is fostered by Feinberg's pass/fail cur-riculum and small-group learning. After my diverse clinical experiences at the University of Michigan–Ann Arbor and now as a hospitalist scribe, I am eager to start clinical training in medical school, so I am excited for the early and integrated clinical experi-ences that begin in phase one. Research was an important part of my undergraduate experience, and I plan to continue clinical research in medical school and in my career as a physician, so I appreciate the opportunity to pursue individual interests through the longitudinal scholarly concentration. Feinberg's dedication to pursuing intellectual curiosity is an ideal fit for my aspirations to work in academic medicine.

- University of Chicago, Biological Sciences Division, Pritzker School of Medicine: I am looking for a collaborative and noncompetitive learning environment, which is fostered by Pritzker's curriculum and advising societies. I value my extracurricular experiences, and the pass/fail curriculum will also allow me to continue a well-rounded student life.

Research was an important part of my undergraduate experience at the University of Michigan–Ann Arbor, and I plan to continue clinical research in medical school and in my career as a physician, so I appreciate the opportunity to pursue individual interests through the summer research program and scholarly project. Pritzker's dedication to pursuing intellectual curiosity is an ideal fit for my aspirations to work in academic medicine.

- Columbia University College of Physicians and Surgeons: Columbia's mission to provide humanistic medicine ideally reflects the holistic care that I greatly value. I appreciate how opportunities for medical and scientific discovery are embedded within Columbia's curriculum through the Scholarly Project and research electives. These opportunities also establish mentor relationships, which are very important to me. Having taken five years of Spanish, I would like to participate in the Spanish-language immersion program the summer after my first year, as I hope to provide the greatest level of care even when patients do not speak English as a first language. Lastly, I spent a lot of time with Columbia students as an undergraduate, and I know that this university ignites students' passions to learn for the sake of knowledge. I would be honored to be a part of Columbia's integrated community.

- University of Illinois: After my diverse clinical experiences at the University of Michigan–Ann Arbor and as a hospitalist scribe, I am eager to start clinical training in medical school, so I'm very excited for the early exposure to patient care through the Longitudinal Primary Care program. This program also establishes a mentor relationship early on, which I found very valuable as an undergraduate. The numerous hospital affiliations will expose me to diverse patient populations. I am particularly interested in working at Cook County Hospital because it serves a similar population as the county hospital where I volunteered. I believe I could contribute to the patients and program with passion.

- University of Central Florida College of Medicine: I spent my childhood and adolescence in Coral Springs. The state's culture is very well-known to me. I have been informed by Dr. Joe Flaherty, former dean of the University of Illinois at Chicago, that UCF is an excellent program. The technology and state-of-the-art imaging would be excellent preparation for the future, and it is great that UCF works to prepare its students and be a leader in technology, which is so tied to quality medicine. Two of UCF's cornerstone values are diversity and inclusion. As a Latino, an underrepresented group in medicine, these are very important to me. I hope to contribute to UCF and the health care of my patients and add to the Spanish-speaking health-care providers of Florida.

- Loyola University Chicago Stritch School of Medicine: I am currently a senior at Loyola University Chicago, where I have grown and learned for three years under the Jesuit curriculum and values. I am already familiar with the campus as I spent the summer of 2014 performing research in the pathology labs under Dr. Iqbal. Having interacted with current medical students of the program, I took note of their happiness and how pleased they were with the program. I firmly believe in the mission, which focuses on leadership and positively impacting the world through striving for an extraordinary life. I believe the standard of excellence I have experienced during my undergraduate training would fit with the medical program's continuation of that standard. I believe I can contribute to the health of Spanish-speaking patients of Chicago, which is known to have many thriving Latino populations where health can often go underserved due to a lack of qualified bilingual health-care providers.

- George Washington University School of Medicine and Health Sciences: GW is regarded as one of the nation's top medical schools. Attending such an institution and receiving a world-class education would be an honor. GW's emphasis on research is a great professional opportunity. Having experience in both medical and inorganic-chemistry research, my time in the lab is something I value, and I hope to contribute to GW's research program. GW's use of active learning rather than traditional large lectures is a method conducive to my learning style. The opportunity to interact with patients early is something I think will benefit my care of patients in the short and long term. I hope to contribute to the diversity of GW's student body and the well-being of the English- and Spanish-speaking patients of DC.

- Oakland University Williams Beaumont School of Medicine: Attending Oakland and receiving a world-class education would be an honor. Oakland's emphasis on research, and being given the ability to design and execute my own research program, is a wonderful opportunity. Having experience in both medical and inorganic-chemistry research, my time in the lab is something I value, and I hope to contribute to Oakland's research facilities. Oakland's use of the capstone project and encouragement of interacting learning are conducive to my learning style. The opportunity to focus on communication skills and patient encounters semester one is something I think will benefit my care of patients in the short and long term. I hope to contribute to the diversity of Oakland's student body and the well-being of the English- and Spanish-speaking patients of Rochester.

- University of Illinois College of Medicine: UIC is regarded as one of the nation's top medical schools. Attending such an institution and receiving a world-class education would be a culmination of my goals and dreams. I hope to contribute to the

Spanish-speaking population of health-care professionals in Chicago, which is known to have many thriving Latino populations yet remains underserved due to a lack of qualified bilingual speakers. UIC's emphasis on teaching effective communication remains a very important aspect to me. I am also excited to read about the genome work that is going on at the school. I believe UIC will keep me on the cutting edge of medical education. I am also interested in public health, and UIC is well positioned in this area as it is a public institution and connected with the state of Illinois.

- Rush Medical College: Rush Medical College excites me because of its emphasis on community-based learning and recognition of the need for preventative health care in traditionally underserved populations. When I spoke with an M3 medical student, they informed me that this school offers countless outreach and community-service programs that allow students to develop as medical professionals while giving back to the community. I believe my ability to speak fluent Spanish would assist in working with underserved populations. While studying at Rush Medical Center, I would take advantage of the Student Mentor Program and Careers in Medicine Program to gain early clinical exposure. In my personal and professional life, I have seen the debilitating effects of chronic illness and appreciate the need for interdisciplinary preventative medicine. I am eager to learn more about how to keep patients healthy, prevent suffering, and provide the best possible care.

- I first became interested in the Chicago Medical School while talking to a current M1A student. They told me about how impressed they were with the hardworking student body, the interprofessional community clinic, and classes such as physiology, which they enjoyed so much that they decided to become a TA for the class. I then visited the campus with one of the professors to watch a medical-school lecture on the history of medicine. The material was fascinating, the students were engaged, and the learning environment made me excited about the prospect of studying in that open lecture hall. I was shown around the incredible campus, and I asked questions about lectures, programs in the buildings, and the organizations available to the student body. Chicago Medical School at Rosalind Franklin University is my top choice of medical schools because I have interacted with this program and I know that this is an institution where I can reach my full potential and be able to provide my patients with the best quality of care.

- Nova Southeastern University's accelerated medical program provides its students an exceptional undergraduate experience with opportunities to perform research or study abroad, which are opportunities I'd like to explore. NSU fosters their students' independence and commitment to their community by giving them learning opportunities beyond the classroom or NSU campus and encourages students to apply their studies to real-life situations. Other schools with accelerated programs require students to increase their number of classes starting their first year, which limits the students' time that could have been spent gaining valuable experiences volunteering at clinics or performing research. NSU is also unique in that it is one of very few accelerated osteopathic medical programs in the nation. Osteopathic medicine focuses on the way all of the body's systems intertwine and affect one another. Similar to the way any inflection in your hands will affect the structure of a clay sculpture, the body's systems are pieces that must come together seamlessly to create a whole. Osteopathic medicine appeals to someone like me who believes in an emphasis on preventative health, physical manipulation, and holism.

- There are numerous components about FIU that I would enjoy being a part of. The neighborhood HELP initiative by Dr. Joe Greer offers a tangible method to reach out to the underserved and indigent community of south Florida and to emphasize the importance of preventative and primary care to the socioeconomically disadvantaged. FIU's clinical training and affiliation with numerous hospitals also provides excellent hands-on clinical experience. In speaking to an M1 student, they mentioned to me that the curriculum at FIU is well-thought-out. Starting from basic science, each subsequent chapter builds upon the one before it. FIU's mandatory research requirement would also help me further develop my scientific interests. They told me that student-faculty interaction at FIU is also very personal and that the faculty is very interested in its students and is open to suggestions. I believe that such close student-professor interactions would strengthen my ability to be an excellent physician.

- I am attracted to Rush Medical College because it would provide me with access to a diverse patient population throughout my training. I tutor CPS children at Chicago Lights Tutoring each week and volunteer at Almost Home Kids on a regular basis. When I spoke with an M4 medical student, she told me that this school offers countless community-service programs that allow students to develop as medical professionals while giving back to the community. Attending Rush would allow me to continue my involvement as well as become involved with other outreach programs. A clinical fellow in my lab who attended Rush for medical school and completed her residency here informed me that Rush is a great place to learn since the faculty members are so invested in and dedicated to their students. Rush Medical College is my first choice for medical school for many reasons, but primarily because of the quality of education I would receive here.

- The reason I want to attend the University of Missouri at Kansas City's accelerated medical program is because it integrates medical classes and clinical experiences from the beginning of the program, which demonstrates the school is committed to its students' success and quality patient care. The docent program is unique to UMKC; by partnering with a docent, students apply their studies in clinics and treatment together. By the time students graduate, they will have more clinical experience and patient interaction than most other medical students will have. This will prepare students to provide higher-quality patient care. The school also distributes the medical classes to take place over six years rather than four, which I believe allows the student more time and opportunities to further understand the subject matter. UMKC has developed a great model of education for a successful outcome of physicians prepared to provide the best possible patient care.

• One aspect that has drawn me to Oakland University William Beaumont School of Medicine is its commitment to community engagement and the opportunities it provides students through the COMPASS program. I have been inspired by working alongside emergency-room physicians as an emergency-room hospital scribe in a lower-income socioeconomic community. I want to be involved in community health in some fashion throughout my medical career. I also want to be a part of the student-centered approach that includes the PRISM mentoring program and the caring faculty. In my daily life, I try to create collaborative environments with my peers, and I look forward to team-based learning with similarly compassionate students. The final attraction I have to OUWB is its clinical training at premier facilities—from the level-one trauma center at Beaumont Royal Oaks to the clinical-skills center at Beaumont Troy.

• One aspect that has drawn me to the Medical College of Wisconsin–Milwaukee is its community mission to serve Wisconsin's most critical health needs. I have been inspired by working alongside emergency-room physicians as an emergency-room hospital scribe in a lower-income socioeconomic neighborhood. I want to be involved in community health in some fashion throughout my medical career. Completing my scholarly pathway in urban and community health would also provide me a personalized education while helping me achieve my career goals. I'm drawn to the discovery curriculum because I'm open-minded about specialties, and I look forward to being exposed to many areas of medicine. The final attraction I have to this school is the opportunity to have early clinical experience at some of the top hospitals in the country.

• One aspect that has drawn me here is UC Irvine's focus on leading the nation in translational medicine. Having the Ultrasound in Medicine program integrated throughout all four years of medical school is an incredible example of this. I am also drawn here by the nationally ranked medical center and the state-of-the-art facilities, including the simulation center. These, combined with dedicated and caring faculty, create an environment where students thrive. I have been inspired by working alongside emergency-room physicians as an emergency-room hospital scribe in a lower-income socioeconomic community. I want to continue to be involved in community health in some fashion throughout my medical career. Volunteering at the UC Irvine outreach clinic would give me valuable experience treating patients who have nowhere else to go for care.

- One aspect that has drawn me here is Quinnipiac's focus on training physicians to be interprofessional team members. Learning alongside nursing and health-science students would be an incredible opportunity, and it would prepare me to give the highest-quality care to patients. I have been inspired by working alongside emergency-room physicians as an emergency-room hospital scribe in a lower-income socioeconomic community. I want to be involved in community health in some fashion throughout my medical career. This school offers many community-service and outreach programs that I would love to be a part of, including the program that provides on-site health care to migrant farmworkers. Other aspects that have drawn me here are the opportunities to have early clinic experience and to be paired with a primary-care preceptor starting in the first semester.

- One aspect that has drawn me here is Saint Louis University's focus on training physicians in humanistic medicine. I have been inspired by working alongside emergency-room physicians as an emergency-room hospital scribe in a lower-income socioeconomic neighborhood. I want to be involved in community health in some fashion throughout my medical career. Volunteering at the Health Resource Center and Casa de Salud would give me valuable experience treating patients who have nowhere else to go for care. Being involved in various learning communities, including service advocacy and global health, would allow me to personalize my education while working with peers with similar passions. I am also drawn here because of the incredible research opportunities at the state-of-the-art Doisy Research Center.

- As a PA student, one has roughly two to three years to become a highly knowledgeable, well-trained health-care provider. So I want to be part of a program that I feel has the resources to prepare me to become the best PA possible in that short period of time. I truly feel Rush is that program. I like the fact that Rush offers an extra nine months of advanced practice rotations. I feel this will provide me with an incredible opportunity to solidify my clinical skills and prepare me to be an incredibly well-trained PA coming out of the program. I'm also fascinated with the practitioner-teacher model implemented here.

- This school is one of the top medical schools in the country with a challenging curriculum and renowned teachers. U of I's Center for Global Health allows me the ability to continue pursuing a career in global health and provides several opportunities to gain international experience, all of which I value in a medical school.

- Rush is a school that is known for its development of good clinical physicians. In my medical-school research, I was looking for schools that would best prepare me for a career in primary-care medicine. What really drew my attention to Rush was the Rush Community Service Initiatives Program. The variety of programs to participate in is impressive. On the website I saw many clinical and nonclinical programs, as well as the option for students to establish a new program or develop a project within the program. I like that these programs are designed to help in underserved communities. Working in the ER this year has shown me that understanding and treating patients from these communities can be challenging. Increased exposure to culturally diverse communities will make my provision of care better. This program also speaks well of the Rush medical community. Although community service is optional, more than 80 percent of students are participants in the program. I am looking to be part of a community that is enthusiastic and interactive. This program seems like a great way to get to know faculty members, students, and other members of the community while doing something that is good for society.

- I have been privileged to have received Jesuit education for the past eight years at Loyola Academy and Georgetown and would love to attend a medical school with the Jesuit learning philosophy. Talking with my friends who have not had the same opportunity, I know there is something special that comes with the Jesuit philosophy of education. Receiving my training at Loyola will give me more than medical knowledge and procedural adequacy. The Jesuit values of commitment to justice and love will give me the foundation I need to not lose sight of the humanity of each patient. I am drawn to Loyola because of its emphasis on empathy for and connection to our fellow person. I hope to improve the medical experience for patients by integrating this philosophy into my practice.

As far as Loyola's campus features, I am intrigued and excited about the collaborative learning center. From what I understand, it has a six-bed virtual hospital that will be built like a clinical-skills hospital and a simulated home-care environment. I read that the building is supposed to be completed by the beginning of next year, and I would be thrilled to have an opportunity to do full hospital simulations before rotations. I like the idea of medical students, nursing students, and others studying to be health-care professionals working together and sometimes independently in a controlled environment to simulate hospital situations. This building would be extremely helpful in developing and refining my clinical skills and learning how to collaboratively work with peers in the hospital.

- I really like Case Western's clinical affiliates—the University Hospitals' Level I Adult and Pediatric Trauma centers will provide a large and varied exposure during clinical rotations. Also, I'm quite interested in several of the combined-degree programs offered at Case, including the PhD in health-care management and the MBA. Plus, I've heard amazing things about the school, its professors, and its teaching style from an MIT alumna who's an M3 at your school. Finally, I'm quite excited about Case Western's curriculum. I consider myself a very self-directed learner, and the WR2 curriculum and case inquiries sound like an amazing way to learn.

- Rush would be my first choice for medical school because of the many advantages that it offers. They have both academic and community physicians. I have spoken to my brother and some of his friends, and they have told me how approachable the teachers are and how participatory the classes are at Rush. Everyone whom I have spoken with who attended Rush Medical School seemed to enjoy the relationships with their professors, as well as the varied clinical experiences that were offered. I'm very interested in the Rush Community Service Initiatives Program. Volunteer work is a big part of my life, and the ability to continue doing it through Rush will be a great privilege. Also, the advances in medicine people at Rush are working toward are fascinating. One of my brother's friends is currently doing research with the head of the Oncology Department. She injects strands of DNA with vaccines and exposes them to cancer cells to see the effects in the hope of finding vaccines to prevent cancer. I would love to get the opportunity to participate in research such as this. Although the professors and the other students are the most important things, I'm very impressed Rush scored so high in *US News & World Report*. I think it would be exciting to work at a new building at Rush.

- Rush: I want to go to Rush for a variety of reasons. First, I am so comfortable at Rush. Having gone to medical school there, I know the staff, the hospital, the residents, and the computer system. I know the strengths, and I also know that I will get great training at Rush. One of the most important things about Rush is that the residents are working directly with the subspecialists managing a wide variety of patients. There are no fellows to act as go-betweens. Also there is a lot of interesting pathology that I have seen at Rush. There are also a lot of bread-and-butter peds, which is important because I plan on becoming a general pediatrician. Finally, Rush has a great outpatient clinic. The attendings there are wonderful. They are always accessible, patient, and willing to teach whenever they get the chance. It's also the busiest outpatient clinic of the city hospitals, so that will help hone my skills for the future.

- Lutheran: There are many things that drew me to Lutheran when I did my rotation there in the NICU. First off, the new facilities are incredible. Yacktman is pristine, and the patient rooms are amazing. Lutheran has a really busy census, and I am looking for a program that is busy. Having said that, the residents do not seem overworked, and they are all friendly and eager to teach. They helped me out in the NICU but also let me have independence with my own patients. They weren't constantly looking over my shoulder. In addition, the outpatient clinic is tremendously busy with wonderful attendings that are eager to teach and are great role models. This will be beneficial because I want to do outpatient general pediatrics.

- Loyola: There are many things that drew me to Loyola. First off, it has a community hospital feel to it. The classes are small, and it seems that the residents and attendings are very close to one another. Another aspect that appealed to me was the curriculum. The wide variety of experiences that the residents get is broader than other programs. For example, during the first year, there are only four inpatient months and months on cardiology, adolescent medicine, and even surgery or anesthesia. Other programs have a higher emphasis on inpatient wards, so since I want to do outpatient medicine, this will benefit me greatly. I like all the simulations and crash courses that are offered so that we can practice our practical skills. I have not had the opportunity to do as many procedures as I have wanted during medical school, and this will be a great opportunity to do them.

- Rainbow Babies: There are many things that drew me to Rainbow. First off, it's at the forefront of technology and has amazing facilities to provide the best patient care. In addition, it is extremely busy. The outpatient clinic and the inpatient clinic are always teeming with patients, and this provides a great way to learn pediatrics. Also, it will help prepare me for life as a general pediatrician in a busy practice. One thing that particularly caught my eye was the emphasis of education on the part of the residents. I have always loved teaching. I was a TA in college and as a fourth-year student have tried to teach the third-year students as much as I could when they were on my service. I hope one day to have medical students work in my office and teach them as much as I can.

- U of A: There are many things that drew me to U of A. First off, I really like the small class size. It gives residents more autonomy when caring for the patient and makes them step into the physician role earlier than in larger programs. Also, I really like the diverse patient population at U of A. I minored in Spanish and really want to improve that aspect of my care. I can effectively communicate with patients now but want to be at a level where I don't need to call a translator on complicated cases. Another area that interests me is desert medicine. I really enjoy being outdoors, and wilderness and adventure medicine has always interested me. Finally, the Global Health Initiative is something I have always wanted to participate in.

- UCLA: One thing that immediately drew me to UCLA were the different training sites that residents work at. The different sites allow for the "total package" when learning peds. At Mattel you do subspecialty work, at Cedars Sinai there is more traditional peds, and at UCLA–Santa Monica there is a mix of the two. Working at each place with its unique patient population and different pathology allows for a well-rounded experience in all aspects of general peds. The patient population that UCLA serves is very important to me. I really want to enhance my Spanish-speaking skills to better serve that population. The large class size is also an advantage because it allows the opportunity to work as a team and learn something from each resident. One thing I really liked was that even though it is a big class, all the residents know each other, and you don't feel lost in the crowd.

- Stanford: One of my friends is a first-year resident there, and the thing she loves most about Stanford is that it has a small-program feel even though it's a relatively large program. There are multiple sites to work at, and each one has its positives. The community outreach is what drew me to Stanford the most, especially since I'm leaning toward specializing in primary care. There is such a good balance of subspecialty work with primary care that each resident gets the best training and is ready to excel in pediatrics upon graduating.

- Oregon: One of the things that drew me to Oregon was the size of their program. With only fifteen residents in a class, it seems like there is individualized attention between residents and attendings, which will help foster each resident in his or her career. Also, the hospital has a large census and thus provides a lot of independent work for each resident. One of the most important things for residents is to learn how to handle patients on their own because when they are done with their residency, they won't have attendings to fall back on. I pride myself on being able to handle patients by myself without the help of senior classmates, so I welcome the opportunity to work with a large and complicated patient load. Also, it seems like there is a large emphasis on resident well-being, and Oregon has both mountain and ocean, which provides a great outlet for things to do when not in the hospital.

- SLU: The first thing that drew me to SLU was the CARE program. During medical school, I volunteered at a free clinic called NLVS, which served mostly the underserved South Asian community. This was one of the clinics in which we were to work, and the most frustrating thing was that we only needed a $25,000 budget to operate for one full year, offering both free prescription medications and basic lab services, while other clinics were operating on multimillion-dollar budgets. It was really an eye-opener to see how people couldn't even afford their diabetes medicine because it was more important for them to feed their families. I feel that the CARE program will help and is a great way to show future physicians how to handle barriers to health care. In the future I want to volunteer at free clinics to help provide care for less fortunate families. In addition, I really like the size of the program, which allows close interaction between attendings and residents. Coming from a smaller medical school, I think a small residency program fits my personality best.

- Children's: The thing that drew me to Children's was the opportunity to work in one of the most prestigious programs and hospitals in the country. Children from all over the world go to Children's for the quality of their care. This allows the residents to see the most unique pathology and routine pathology presenting in different ways. However, even though there are a lot of rare cases, there are a lot of bread-and-butter pediatrics that happen in the hospital, and it is this blend of common and rare that will benefit me most in my practice. Also, there is a strong emphasis on outpatient medicine, which I am leaning toward. Half the graduates end up working in general pediatrics, and with all the subspecialty training, I will feel more comfortable handling these cases myself rather than referring to a specialist.

SO, YOU
WANT TO BE
A PHYSICIAN

C H A P T E R   1 2

TYPICAL QUESTIONS ASKED DURING INTERVIEWS

QUESTIONS PROVIDED BY PRIOR STUDENTS:

- Tell me about yourself.
- Why do you want to be a physician?
- What first made you interested in medicine?
- Who has been a major inspiration in your choice of medicine?
- Why do you want to come to _____ for medical school?
- What do you like about this school's program?
- What do you believe is the purpose of medical school?
- What do you think will be the most difficult part of medical school for you?
- What do you hope to gain from this experience?
- What do you do to de-stress?
- How will you / how do you handle stress?
- How do you overcome stress?
- What do you do when you get frustrated?
- How do you handle change?
- How will you / how do you handle disappointment?
- Define empathy.
- Define compassion.
- What makes having compassion or being compassionate important?
- How can you effectively deal with someone in crisis?
- Define failure.
- How do you address failure?
- Please give me an example of a time when you have failed.

- Define success.
- What process do you use in making important decisions?
- From a professional standpoint, what are the negative aspects of medicine?
- What are some of the problems facing health care today?
- What is the most important issue in health care today?
- Tell me about your community service.
- What experiences have you had in community involvement that demonstrate your commitment to the practice of medicine?
- What are your specific goals in medicine?
- What are your hobbies? What do you do in your spare time?
- What is your favorite activity?
- What do you do for fun?
- What is your ideal day?
- Where have you enjoyed traveling?
- What are your accomplishments?
- How do you think your background will impact your practice?
- Describe yourself and your work ethic.
- Would a career in academic medicine interest you?
- Do you prefer working in a research environment or with people?
- What do you think makes a good doctor? Why would you be a good doctor?
- What are your greatest challenges? (Then followed up with questions specific to my response.)
- What are your strengths?
- What are your weaknesses?
- If you could change one aspect of your personality, what would it be?
- What aspects of your life experiences would make you a good candidate for our school?
- Describe your research in layman's terms. Would you consider doing this during your residency?
- What do you think about HMOs and PPOs?
- How would your career plans change if you knew that in the future all doctors would be working in HMOs?
- How would a national health-insurance plan affect the physician and the patient?
- What is the difference between Britain's health-care delivery system and ours?
- What would you like to add to your application?
- How will you finance your medical education?
- Describe your current living conditions.

- Why dentistry?
- What exposure do you have to dentistry?
- How have you reached out to the community and educated people about oral health?
- What is a challenge you have faced, and how did you handle it?
- Describe a time you have worked in a group. How did you deal with the different personalities?
- Describe your communication style.
- Describe your personality.
- Describe a time when you had to utilize effective interpersonal skills.
- Describe a time when you were dependable or showed initiative.
- Describe a time when you have been disappointed in a teammate. What happened, and how did you approach the situation?
- Have you had any experience being in a group where there were differing races, cultures, or religions, and how were you able to navigate through those differences? What did you learn?
- Describe cultural diversity in your life and why it is important to you.
- Would you practice medicine in the inner city? How do you think working in that environment would impact you as a physician?
- How do you function within a group? As a leader or follower?
- What does it mean to be a leader for you?
- Describe a time in which you took on a leadership role.
- How do you prioritize your time if you have many things to do?
- Describe a time you went beyond expectations.
- Discuss a time when you were misjudged and how you overcame it.
- How do you think you can apply your interests to being a better physician?
- If you could invite any four people to dinner, who would they be? Why?
- What roles do you associate with a physician? (Educator, healer...)
- What qualities do you look for in a physician?
- What was the main event or experience that convinced you that you wanted to be a physician?
- Where do you see yourself in ten years? Please be specific— for example, practicing in a private office, hospital...
- Discuss your strengths and how those pertain to practicing medicine.
- Based on your shadowing experiences, what would you mirror from the physicians you observed, and what would you try to not mirror?
- What questions do you have about the program?
- Tell me about your family background and how that has shaped your life.
- What do you do on the weekend before a big test?

- Why community health?
- Tell me about your volunteering and the scholarship you won.
- What have you done to improve your GPA, because there is such a difference between beginning of college and end of college?
- If you could begin college again, what would you do differently?
- What was your undergraduate major? How did you choose it?
- What extracurricular activities were you involved in during your undergraduate years?
- Which accomplishments in your college career are most memorable for you?
- Tell me about your MCAT score.
- Explain a time when you had to make a really important decision quickly with little information.
- Do you feel that the government should fund more dental students, law students, or engineering students than any other students? State pros and cons.
- How can you overcome the conflicts that are associated with being a doctor?
- Why is UMKC a major school on your list?
- What area in medicine do you want to major in and why? Do you have a specialty in mind?
- What subspecialty do you see yourself pursuing? Why?
- Who has motivated you to become involved with science?
- How can you keep up with a six-year BA/MD program?
- How can you make a difference in patients' lives?
- What are the key things a doctor must have? What makes a good doctor?
- How has volunteering at the hospital been significant for you?
- Tell me about your current job.
- Go into more detail about the research paper you mention on your application.
- We have hundreds of applicants as qualified as you. What is it about you that should make us choose you over them?
- Did your parents ever try talking you out of pursuing medicine?
- What can you bring to medicine?
- Do you believe practicing medicine would be a rewarding experience?
- How do you handle gore and blood?
- Why are you a good fit for Loyola?
- Tell us what you think of our curriculum.
- What will you do if you do not get into medical school this year?
- Have you considered other medical fields?
- Have you considered any other health-care professions, specifically nursing or physician assistant?
- If you cannot be a doctor, what will you do?

- Talk about a time when you had difficulty adjusting to a situation. Why did you have difficulty?
- What is your greatest achievement?
- Talk about a challenge that you had to overcome.
- Tell me about your high school.
- I see you went to Adlai Stevenson High School; please tell me what you know about Adlai Stevenson.
- I see you went to John Kennedy High School; please tell me what you know about John Kennedy.
- I see you went to Dwight Eisenhower High School; please tell me what you know about Dwight Eisenhower.
- Tell me more about your time in Japan.
- Describe your level of exposure to other cultures here and around the globe.
- Is studying abroad something that is still important to you? Why?
- Tell me more about what you have been doing recently.
- Medical school is a marathon; how will you make it through?
- How important are your social support systems?
- Tell me about your path to get here.
- Tell me more about your past work experiences.
- Which newspapers or journals do you regularly read?
- What are your career plans, and what led you to the decision to become a physician?
- Where do you see yourself (medically / as a physician) in twenty years?
- How would your role as a doctor fit in with your role as a member of the community?
- How will you maintain a fresh understanding of community needs?
- Do you think that medical students who receive federal loans should spend time practicing medicine in a rural or inner-city area to give society something in return?
- How do you feel about health-care reform?
- Are you optimistic or pessimistic about health-care reform?
- What do you think is lacking in our health-care system?
- What are some problems you see in medicine and health care today?
- What is the health-care system like in Hong Kong?
- Is health-care reform on a positive trajectory?
- How are technology and other changes in the world addressing the issues in regard to health-care reform?
- What have you done to acquaint yourself with what a doctor does?
- Please give three words or attributes that describe you.

- If asked to describe you, name three things your friends would say.
- How would your teammates describe you?
- How would your professors describe you?
- How would these attributes make you a good doctor?
- If we contact your references, what do you think they would say about you?
- What are your thoughts about other campuses at the U of I?
- What do you think a typical Northwestern student is?
- What do you have to offer our medical school?
- Which medical schools have you applied to?
- Where do we stand in the list of medical schools you applied to?
- Why do you think so many people want to become doctors?
- What was your favorite college course? What did you enjoy about it?
- If you want to help people, why not choose a career like social work?
- How would you deal with a terminally ill patient?
- Do you think a doctor should tell a patient he or she has ten months to live?
- Is there anything else you would like us to know about you before you leave the interview?

SO, YOU
WANT TO BE
A PHYSICIAN

CHAPTER 13

NEGATIVE/MEAN-SPIRITED INTERVIEW QUESTIONS

Prior to the 2015–16 calendar year, I had never coached any student who had received what I felt was a negative or mean-spirited question. In the 2015–16 school year, I received feedback from every student that I had coached, which was nine, that in all of their interviews, which totaled thirty, they had received (at least what I felt were) negative or mean-spirited questions. I had let my students down because I had not seen questions of this nature before and therefore had not prepared them for questions of this nature. I can't speak for the medical schools because I don't know what they were thinking, but I had assumed that the only potentially negative, mean-spirited question that an interviewee might be asked was, what do you perceive is your biggest weakness? During 2015–16 the questions they asked that I felt were more mean-spirited or negative are as follows:

- Tell me about a time you faced a conflict with another individual. How did you respond?
- What would your best friend describe as your worst trait?
- Tell me about a time when you failed.
- Tell me about a time when you let your team down.
- Tell me about a time when you were criticized unfairly and what you did about it.
- Tell me about the worst thing that ever happened to you.
- Tell me about a time you have disappointed a teammate or a group member.
- Tell me about a time when you hurt someone.
- Tell me about a time when you were the only person in a group who disagreed, and what were the circumstances?
- Tell me about a time when you wanted to help someone who didn't want your help.

- Describe a situation in which you were not as dependable as you would have liked.
- Tell me about a time you had to deal with your own pre-conceived notions or prejudices against someone.
- What was a difficult negative experience you have encountered?
- If I asked someone who doesn't like you about you, what would he or she say?
- Describe a time you were unable to fulfill a task. How did you handle the consequences?
- Why do you think you scored lower on the MCAT than other students who have applied here?

CHAPTER 14

UNIQUE/UNUSUAL
INTERVIEW QUESTIONS

QUESTIONS PROVIDED BY PRIOR STUDENTS:

- What do you think of Obamacare?
- Do you believe that physicians should be in a union?
- In your opinion, who was the most influential person of the last hundred years?
- If you were a cookie, what cookie would you be?
- In which college course did you get the worst grades?
  What made it challenging for you?
- What is your opinion of HMOs and the changes taking place in medicine?
- What do you think about euthanasia?
- What do you think is the most pressing issue in medicine?
- What do you think about the ongoing conflict in Iraq?
- When you need counseling for personal problems, whom do you talk with?
- What is success?
- What nonmedical books have you read recently,
  and why did you chose those books?
- What is your solution to terrorism?
- What is the biggest problem in the world today?
- What do you think about American primary health-care delivery—that
  is, status quo, total private system, national health insurance?
- Say you're on an airplane and the man next to you is start-
  ing to panic at the thought of flying—what would you do?
- What will your obituary say?
- At your college, did you ever feel like a num-
  ber among forty thousand students?
- Do you believe medicine is a science or an art?

- Do you believe in mandated donated service for doctors?
- If you could visit one place in the world, where would it be and why?
- If you could walk on water forever or fly three separate times, which would you choose and why?
- Describe one benefit technology brings to medicine and one negative impact technology may have on medicine.
- "Fun question"...If I gave you a blank canvas, what would you paint?

THE INTERVIEW EXPERIENCE FROM A STUDENT'S PERSPECTIVE

I had my interview with Loyola Stritch School of Medicine, and it went incredibly well. They were very friendly, and the interview style was very laid-back. When I arrived, the people at the admissions office handed me my itinerary for the day, which consisted of two interviews at 9:30 and 11:00 a.m., each one hour long. After that I took a tour with a first-year med student, had lunch, and then sat with some other students for a while in the Medical Center Commons area.

My first interview was with a doctor from the Pediatric Neonatology Unit. He brought me into his office, and we never really went through any formalities. We began talking, and the interview was more of a back-and-forth conversation than a question-and-answer session. I would say he spent just as much time talking as I did. He asked me about my dad, who graduated from Loyola, and we went from there. We covered everything on my application, and most of his questions pertained directly to what he had read on my application. He asked about my trip with Global Medical Brigades, my research with Dr. M., and what kind of doctor I wanted to be. It was very informal, and I could tell he just wanted to get to know me. He did ask why I did not follow my dad's career path into dentistry, and thanks to you I had a great answer prepared. There were no questions that were out of the blue. His question style was along the lines of, "So, tell me about your experience with such-and-such organization."

My second interview was with a resident in the Pediatric Unit. She graduated from U of I, as did my first interviewer. We had a lot in common, and our interview, again, was conversational. She brought me into a room with a small round table in the back of the admissions office, and she began with a question straight off of my application. We talked about similar things that I talked about in my first interview, but we also talked about life outside of school, and she told me how she balances her career with a personal life. She asked about my hobbies and what I like to do outside of the classroom. Again, she took all of her questions straight off of my application, and nothing caught me off guard.

Neither interviewer, at any point, asked me something like, "Tell me about a leadership experience," or, "What makes you special for our school?" I was very nervous leading up to the interview, but I was not nervous at all once the whole process started.

At one point, the head of admissions came and talked with the group of interviewees. He gave us a short rundown of what Loyola is all about and what student life is like. Then he said that Loyola wants students who want to be there, and he asked us each why we chose to apply to Loyola. I had a feeling that he did this with all students who interview, so I would recommend to anyone else applying to Loyola to come up with a good answer to that question. I referred to their mission statement in my answer. I said that Loyola's mission statement says that the school's priorities lie in service, compassion, and respect for human life. I said that when I think of practicing medicine, those are the things that immediately come to mind.

Feedback from Another Student

In the interviews, I was asked the three questions you told me, as well as various random questions, such as what epitaph I would want on my tombstone, what I do for fun, and what will be the biggest challenge I will face in medical school.

Challenging Interview Questions

Increasingly, students are being asked what they think about health-care reform. Despite the Supreme Court's decision, this is an area in which I don't want to provide advice because if a student states an opinion on the issue and the interviewer doesn't agree, the student is in trouble.

Nonetheless—and again, despite the Supreme Court having ruled—here's a question every medical school candidate had better be prepared to answer (and some suggested answers):

• What do you think about Obamacare?

I would recommend considering the following questions and suggested answers:

1. **What is Obamacare? (Please note, only opponents of PPACA refer to the health care reform act by this name.)**

   Answer: It is sweeping health care reform legislation that is complicated and may have unintended consequences. Only time will tell. Key provisions are intended to extend coverage to millions of uninsured Americans, to implement measures that will lower health-care costs while at the same time increasing quality and efficiency, and to eliminate insurance-industry practices such as denial of coverage due to preexisting conditions.

2. **What do Republicans say?**

   Answer: "Obamacare" is unconstitutional due to the individual-mandate provision, which requires all Americans to purchase health insurance. It places an undue burden on small business and will cost Americans more health-care dollars, not less. Congress is overreaching into the private affairs and decisions of American citizens. Recently, when "Obamacare" was challenged in the Supreme Court, the legislation was upheld.

3. What do Democrats say?

Answer: Health care is a fundamental right of all Americans. Since persons who are uninsured are basically cared for on the backs of insured Americans, it is only fair that all persons be required to carry insurance, but it must be made accessible and affordable for Americans on all ends of the economic spectrum. PPACA will save lives, as ample research demonstrates that the uninsured die from every cause at a much higher rate, and health-care reform will begin to control health-care costs.

4. What is a neutral statement?

Answer: I support certain aspects of the act but have reservations about others. For example, I think it is good that more people will have access to insurance, but I worry about the costs. Also, I think that while it is important to make health care more efficient and to have high-quality outcomes, I hope it doesn't interfere with the relationship between doctors and patients. I think all of us will have to work cooperatively over a long period of time to ensure that America's health care remains the best in the world.

If you find yourself in a situation where you must answer, I would recommend a neutral statement.

A corollary question is whether access to quality medical care is a right or a privilege. Again, this is based on the perspective of the interviewer, and I don't see how you can provide a response without the risk of getting into trouble. The most neutral response I can suggest in regard to whether health care is a right or a privilege is to try to land somewhere in the middle. For example, you could say, "I believe that everyone should be able to receive the medical treatment they need, but I understand there are unlimited legitimate needs and limited resources."

Another Good Answer to Yet Another Good Question

- Why didn't you go to medical school directly after graduation?

I have talked with my father often about his medical-school experiences, and from what he tells me, when clinical rotations began in his class, there was a noticeable difference between students who had previous clinical experience and those who did not. He said that he could always tell who had clinical experience because those students were more comfortable and confident in their patient interactions. Although I had experience as an EMT, I wanted more practical experience with doctors. I found a great opportunity to do this with my job as an emergency-room scribe. As a scribe I get to see a variety of interesting medical cases and observe how doctors handle different types of patients. One of the more acute cases I saw was of a mentally retarded infant who came into the ER in critical condition. Due to the infant's age and condition, a group of doctors dropped what they were doing to evaluate the infant and figure how to best handle the delicate situation. The doctor I was scribing for managed to intubate the infant and lower his breathing rate from over sixty breaths per minute to a normal rate. Situations like these show me how I should handle myself when I eventually start clinical rotations.

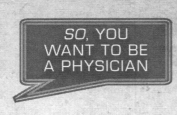

CHAPTER 15

THE MULTIPLE MINI INTERVIEW

Recently, some medical schools have started to shift away from relying entirely on a traditional interview model and now utilize the Multiple Mini Interview (MMI) method. Prospective medical students should expect that there is a possibility that they could be evaluated in this manner. Created by McMaster University, the MMI seeks to test interviewees in ways that can't be as easily prepared for ahead of time. Your personality and critical thinking skills will be the focus in this style of interview. McMaster developed this interview method in hopes that it would ascertain which students would be most successful in medical school and in the field of medicine. Although challenging for some students, others will find this style less challenging.

The MMI will ask you to respond to different scenarios involving questions frequently having to do with ethics and cultural understanding. You will be asked to leave any personal items, such as phones, outside the room. MMI interviews take many forms, as the examples that follow will show.

Although there are six examples that follow, there are generally four main MMI styles that you will likely encounter. One style will give you a scenario that you will discuss with the interviewer. You will need to address how you would respond to the scenario you have been given, and then the interviewer may follow up with additional questions that will delve deeper into your answer. This style might feel similar to a debate, as you may find yourself being asked to clarify and defend your stance.

Role-play interview scenarios are another very common type of MMI station style and will involve an actor who usually plays the part of a patient, patient's family member, or medical colleague. You must interact with the actor and respond to his or her role within the scenario you have been given. Be prepared, as these encounters can be intense and cover tough emotional ground, such as role-play where you have to tell a patient he or she has a terminal disease.

Another type of MMI interview involves working with another candidate or candidates. You will perform a task together while observed by the interviewer. You may work together, or one student may be asked to help direct the other candidate in the task. The tasks will most likely be relatively straightforward, but the way in which you face challenges and your ability to work well with others will be the focus here.

The last format is more typical of a traditional interview style and will be between you and an interviewer. This style will allow you to utilize what you have learned from the Goldberg Method for interviewing. Although the questions for the MMI stations often will change from year to year, you very well may be able to prepare in advance for this MMI style, as you would for a traditional interview.

Although medical schools may be looking for slightly different traits in their candidates, they will likely be looking at how well you perform in the areas of intellect, team cooperation, empathy, ethics, insight, integrity and principles, cultural understanding, professionalism, ability to communicate effectively, and the strength of your organizational and problem-solving skills during your MMI scenarios. The interviewers will be looking for you to be confident in your decisions and stances and defend your opinion and understanding of the situation. They will also be monitoring how you perform under stress, as well as your abilities in verbal and nonverbal communication.

Medical ethics issues will be a focus in the MMI scenarios, and the scenarios themselves may be quite varied. Expect ethical scenarios relating to autonomy, justice, beneficence, and nonmaleficence. Autonomy scenarios will relate to a patient's rights and how he or she wishes to be treated. Justice involves fairness in the distribution of health care and resources. Beneficence expects that doctors will make decisions based on their patient's best interests. Nonmaleficence addresses your responsibility to ensure that you don't harm patients entrusted to your care. Although these address common ethical scenarios presented in the MMI interviews, please understand that the interviewers are not expecting you to have the medical knowledge and understanding of a physician. They just want a thoughtful answer.

Examples of Actual MMI Interviews

In the 2014–15 school year, I coached eight students who had forty interviews. None of the students had an MMI interview. The number of interviews in this year was skewed because one student had eighteen interviews.

In the 2015–16 school year, I coached nine students who had a total of thirty interviews, of which six of the students had an MMI interview. I expect the number of MMI interviews may continue to increase in the future. It was for this reason, among others, that I felt the book required an update.

Of the six students who had an MMI interview in the 2015–16 school year, each indicated that they had a regular one-on-one interview and an MMI interview, and each of their MMIs were different.

One student indicated that there were several stations and they were given five minutes to answer questions such as the following:

- "What would you do if a coworker was making racial slurs?"
- "What would you do if classmates were making inappropriate posts online about the school, faculty members, and patients?"
- "Do you think diversity and socioeconomic status, culture, religion, and background should play a role in medical-school admissions?"
- "What experiences encouraged you to pursue medicine?"

Another student indicated that there were twelve stations and they were given five minutes to answer each question. Some of these questions were as follows:

- "If you have the choice of giving a transplant to a successful elderly member of the community or a twenty-year-old drug addict, how do you choose?"
- "Discuss a book you have read for pleasure recently. Why did you select that book?"
- "A twenty-three-year-old patient who has been in an accident needs a blood transfusion. She states that her religion doesn't allow this. You are the physician in charge. What will you do? Will you override the objection? Why or why not?"

The next student indicated that there were multiple stations and outside each station there was a prompt for the student to read and quickly think of a response indicating what to do in that situation. The student then entered the room and responded to the prompt. After responding, the student might be asked additional questions. Each station was timed for four minutes, and there was a bell that indicated that it was time to move on to the next station. Some of the questions asked of this student were as follows:

- "Teach me something."
- "What are the three most memorable experiences in your life?"
- "What three wishes would you ask a genie to grant you?"
- "What are some ways you can use a quarter without spending it?"
- "What three things would you bring on a desert island?"

Another student was given two minutes to prepare for a six-minute interview, with a total of eleven different stations. The stations are listed as follows:

- Four stations presented ethical scenarios.
- Two stations were collaborative, and the student worked with another candidate to reproduce an image.
- Two stations asked the student to tell the interviewer how specific quotes resonated with them.
- Two stations asked the student to draw upon his or her past experience to explain why he or she wanted to be a physician.
- One station asked a miscellaneous question about the student's background.

Another student was given a card with a particular scenario on it and had two minutes to read and consider how to respond. After the two minutes passed, the student was invited into the room and had eight minutes to address the scenario. The card instructed the student in their role in the scenario before they encountered it. The questions were not meant to assess their medical knowledge but rather test how they handled challenges. They were not able to have a discussion with the interviewer, but they could ask questions if they needed clarification regarding the scenario. They did not have a lot of time between the stations, so these fast-paced interviews tried to uncover their true nature and character when encountering high-pressure situations, with little time to process them. Some of these situations were as follows:

- One of your patients is in a coma and is on life support. You have had several different specialists come in to evaluate the patient, and they all report that the patient's condition is not going to improve and that the patient is brain-dead. The specialists believe that the patient should be taken off life support, but the family does not want to do that. What do you do in this situation?
- You are an oncologist with a very depressed, possibly suicidal patient. Do you tell your patient that he or she has a serious noncurable cancer, and if so, how?

The final student, after their one-to-one session, was assigned to one of four separate groups of students. Each group was assigned a separate question:

- "How do you overcome difficulties?"
- "What are the characteristics of a compassionate physician?"
- "What is the biggest problem facing health care?"
- "Why do college freshmen seem unprepared for college-level work?"

The groups worked together, and there was a medical-school physician and a medical student who sat quietly over each group and watched them interact, come to a consensus, and respond to each question.

So, as can be seen above, there does not seem to be a standard use of the MMI. Although the sample is very small, the majority being five out of six, students were asked questions individually at a station, given a time limit, and then moved on after their response. In one case they were divided into a group and asked to work together as a group to answer a question.

Ethical Questions

When I first started this process nine years ago, it seemed like many medical schools asked the same ethical question over and over again: what would you do if you saw a student cheating? If it were me, I would say I would mind my own business, but that's not the politically correct answer. The politically correct answer is, "I would confront the person and say that if he or she didn't admit to cheating, then I would have to report him or her."

Another example of an ethical question one of my students was asked went something like this: Your future husband's parents have never liked you and don't want their son to marry you. You have a difficult time with them, and two weeks before your wedding ceremony, they send you an extremely expensive mahogany bedroom set, dining-room set, and living-room set. What do you say to your in-laws? My response would have been, "Thank you very much." Then the medical-school interviewer says, "Well, I'm going to tell you that mahogany is a banned and it's against the law to utilize it. Now what would you tell your in-laws?" My response would be, "Well, if I refuse it, it's not going to grow back in the rain forest, so I would simply make a donation within my means to the organization that saves mahogany or the rain forest." Would this have satisfied the interviewer? I don't know. Below are other examples of ethical questions to consider.

1. You are working as a resident, and a doctor tells you to order tests for a patient. You realize two hours later, after other tests come back, that you left out one of the tests that the doctor told you to order. You have had a lot of experience with these types of patients and know what the course of action to treat the patient will be and that the lab test that was left out is not required. What do you do?

2. A patient goes to the doctor for a regular checkup, and the patient tells him about some problem he has been having (chest pain). Due to the patient's family history and complaint, the doctor tells the patient, who is a heavy smoker, that he has to

quit smoking. You document this in the medical record. The patient is uncooperative and does not stop. Smoking helps him relieve the stress he has from working two jobs to support his wife and eight kids. Sometime later, the patient files a malpractice lawsuit against the doctor because a blood clot was discovered in his leg. The patient blames the doctor for not making him quit smoking. How would you have acted as a physician to make sure the patient quit smoking?

3. Discuss a time when you have had an ethical dilemma.

4. You're late to surgery clinic due to bad weather, and the attending has already excised a site. She tells you to close on your own and leaves the room. After you finish suturing, you realize that the site is the wrong one. What do you do?

5. Under what circumstances would you consider stealing a loaf of bread? What are the cons? What can a person steal in modern times that would be comparable to bread?

6. How can you overcome the ethics of medicine within the coming years?

7. How do you address a financial situation with a poor patient and a rich patient?

8. Do you judge a patient?

9. Do you believe in giving a placebo to a patient?

10. One of your patients is in a coma and is on life support. You have had several different specialists come in to evaluate the patient, and they all report that the patient's condition is not going to improve. The specialists believe that the patient should be taken off life support, but the family does not want to do that. What do you do in this situation?

The key to these MMI interviews is to be honest, caring, and thoughtful. Try to consider the scenario from all angles, and answer clearly and confidently. Here are a few tips to focus on in preparation for your MMI interviews:

• Before you arrive for your MMI interview, review and practice the answers you prepared for the "three questions," and other practice questions, by utilizing the Goldberg Method described in chapter 11. This will help you be prepared for the traditional MMI section.

- Read up on medical ethics and find examples of ethical dilemmas within the field of medicine. Seek out sample MMI questions online or in books, and then place as many questions and scenarios as you can on note cards. Make some of the questions easy, but test yourself with more difficult situations. The more difficult the scenarios become in practice, the more likely you will gain confidence in your ability to respond to any question thrown at you in the MMI format.
- Ask a parent or friend to test you on the ethical dilemmas while being timed. This should help you to prepare to respond quickly during timed MMI scenarios.
- Engage in role-playing exercises, and ask for feedback from those who are working with you. Did you demonstrate empathy? Did you sound confident? Do you understand the larger issues? If you are concerned with getting genuine feedback from your friends and family, you may choose to record yourself or ask a professor or coach to work with you in developing these skills.
- Review your interview etiquette, and make sure to practice your eye contact, handshake, posture, and greeting.
- Be yourself! Be genuine! You have done all you can to prepare!

WANT TO BE
A PHYSICIAN

CHAPTER 16

CASPER

In 2017, some medical schools started to utilize a new test called CASPer. CASPer is a timed exam which students take using their computer. All of my students in 2017 have been asked to take this test for some of the medical schools they have applied to. They all have the same feedback, which is that the timeframe provided to complete the exam is challenging.

You can expect to be provided with a scenario or a question in which you will need to answer one of several ethical and critical thinking questions, as well as queries concerning communication skills and knowledge of health care. My 2017 students indicated that none of the CASPer questions they were asked were healthcare related, and were more focused on situational interpersonal issues and the communication, skills, compassion and ingenuity required to address them.

For example, you may watch a short video where a doctor informs their patient that they have a communicable disease. The patient feels they can keep this condition a secret, and take precautions to minimize the risk of spreading the disease. The partner of this patient also happens to be a patient of the doctor's.

1. Should the doctor inform the unaware partner?
2. Are there grounds for the doctor to discontinue treating their patient, if the patient refuses to comply with the doctor's instructions?
3. What other options does the physician have?

Be careful in answering these questions. For example, if you say the doctor should inform the unaware patient, that would be a HIPPA violation of confidentiality.

Another example of the type of scenario you could be presented with on a CASPer test could be similar to the following:

A patient was found unconscious on the street with no family members present, and a passerby called fire rescue. The patient was brought to the emergency department in an extremely critical condition and was intubated and placed on a ventilator in the ICU. The patient had no insurance. The on call primary care physician called in a neurologist as a consultant who performed an EEG on day one, day four and day six of the hospitalization. Each of the EEG's showed flat lines showing no signs of brain activity. The neurologist indicated that the patient was legally brain dead and called in a second consultation of a different neurologist who concurred. The patient was not conscious and did not have a spouse or power of attorney. He had four children, none of whom had power of attorney, and it was Day 10 of the hospitalization.

Three of the four children had visited their father once and one had visited twice. Two of the children were demanding that the hospital do whatever they can to save their father, even though they were told by the attending physician and a neurologist that their father was legally brain dead. All four of the children said they would not help with the finances in any manner what so ever. The other two children felt that they should take their father off the ventilator to let him die with dignity and peace. Please answer the following questions in regard to this scenario.

1. Should the primary care physician communicate to all four children, not only the futility of their father's medical condition, but the painful nature of what the patient is going through?
2. Should the primary care physician try to have the four children agree to take their father off the ventilator and allow him to die with dignity?
3. In what circumstances could a physician ask for the hospital's legal help?
4. In what circumstances could the physician ask the courts to intervene?
5. Are payment issues a factor in making a decision?

A good way to try to prepare as much as possible for this type of test is to create or find ethical and critical thinking questions and answers, and seek to build your knowledge of health care and communication skills. More information on CASPer, and a link for sample CASPer questions, is provided below. Time yourself answering these questions, with the goal of being to be able to answer all questions in the provided time frame. You will need to be succinct, and as with everything related to these interviews, practice and preparation are key.

More about CASPer: https://takecasper.com/aboutcasper/

Take a sample CASPer test: http://go.takecasper.com/s3/Sample-CASPer-2015

CHAPTER 17
RECEIVING YOUR DESIRED RESIDENCY

Your Trip

Each of you began the trip to finding the residency of your choice many years ago by having the right grade point average, the right community or health-related experiences, the right ACT score in high school, and by selecting what college you wanted to go to and which college would accept you. You studied hard in college, perhaps performing research and doing well on the MCATs, and subsequently decided which medical school you wanted to go to and which would accept you (again, not necessarily the same), and then strived to perform well in medical school. Now it will depend upon how well you perform on the National Boards.

Knowing Your Specialty

Another important factor is to know what specialty you want to be in. I've talked to many medical students in their second year, and they say they really don't know what specialty they desire—they're thinking of this, they're thinking of that, but they're not sure. I certainly understand their ambivalence; however, if you know what you want and how to get there—you're much more likely to find it.

Elective Rotations

Those individuals who know the specialty they desire should make certain that they receive as many elective clinical rotations in that specialty at teaching hospitals as they can find. This is where the friendships you've made with your professors will pay off big. If your professors have a friend in that residency program or in that medical school, they might be able to write a letter or, better yet, give a phone call on your behalf. The bottom line is that if you know what you want to do, take all of your optional elective rotations in that specialty at teaching hospitals that offer that specialty if you can get them.

If you are lucky enough to get one, make sure you're the first one there and the last to leave. Additionally, make sure that you don't look like a goody-goody and ask five questions every day but rather get in there early and stay late or come in early and look at something unique from one of the patients you're going to perform rounds on the next day and think about a very intelligent question. For example, say a patient has been in the hospital five times over the past three years with numerous infections and his or her hemoglobin is slightly reduced but not much below normal. The patient's mother had chronic lymphocytic leukemia, and his or her lymph nodes are slightly enlarged. You may wish to suggest to the attending that there's a possibility that the patient has some type of large B-cell lymphoma. You should respectfully ask whether he or she should order a CT scan and an IgM, IgA, or IgG to see if there are signs of a lymphoma. The point is to be prepared to answer all questions, know the patients you're going to round on in advance, and ask one good intelligent question once a week. Be like Columbo: ask questions you know the answer to. Don't be a goody-goody or a quiet mouse.

The Most Important Thing Is to Be Nice to Everybody

The most important thing, is, when you're doing your elective rotations, make sure that you're nice to everybody, and I mean everybody. Everybody. Every nurse, every volunteer, every house-keeper, every food-service worker, every other person doing his or her rotations with you, all of the attendings, and particularly the residency adviser, although the residency advisers can be influenced by the other individuals that I mentioned. Say hi or hello to everyone you meet. Write thank-you notes at the end of your rotation thanking all of the attendings and the residency director and any other physicians or staff that were helpful. Additionally, find the best German bakery you can, or if not that then the best bakery in town, and get two or three coffee cakes for everybody—the residents, the attendings, the nurses, the secretaries, and so on—with a personal note saying, "Thank you so much for helping me during my rotation. It was a wonderful experience getting to learn so much and to work with such kind and helpful people."

Your hope is that they will remember you in a positive fashion and that you'll subsequently do well enough on your Boards that they will select you when it's time for a residency. I can tell you that if they have a medical student from Northwestern who scored in the ninetieth percentile on the National Boards but did not do a rotation there and if you did everything you were supposed to during your rotation and scored a 90 percent on your National Board score after attending a lower-ranked medical school, they will most likely pick you, the one they know and like!

National Boards / Step 1 / Step 2

Please, please, if there's anything you get from this, it's that you need to pay significant time and attention to the National Boards. This will decide more than anything whether you will receive the residency that you desire. Even if your medical school offers a course in preparing for the Boards, please, if it's available, also take the live, in-person course provided by either Kaplan or Princeton in your area (not the online version so that it's convenient for you), as well as the one offered by your school. I have seen so many medical students that have spent time doing community-service activities, working with physicians, and doing other things, and if they had put the same time into studying for the National Boards, they would have had the residency that they desired. Doing the book version or online version is not the same, and by taking Kaplan or Princeton in person, they will actually demonstrate how you're doing at the end of every week. If you demonstrate a weakness, get a tutor!

Personal Statements

Just like you needed to get into medical school, many residency programs will have you write a personal statement. My recommendation is not to be cute and to explain to them that you want to help other people, that you have always enjoyed the sciences, and why you have a particular interest in the specialty you're applying for. Feel free to mention individual things you've specifically learned during your elective rotation in that specialty. Any research you've done in that specialty will also be extremely helpful.

The Interview

By now each of you might think that you know how to interview because you've gone through it in the medical-school process, and if you think what got you into medical school will get you into residency, then I think you should follow your heart and do what you would like to do. If you are open-minded, please listen on.

The Goldberg Method

As discussed in chapter 11, I personally developed my own system called "the Goldberg Method", in which I ask the student to answer three questions: Number one, tell me about yourself. Number two, why do you want to be in this specialty? Number three, why do you want to come to this residency program?

You might ask how I came up with these questions. For the first ninety-one students that I coached, they were typically doctors' sons, daughters, nieces, nephews, or next-door neighbors. Because I was doing the service for free at that time, while being a full-time hospital administrator at eighty-plus hours a week, I asked them (a) if I helped them or not and (b) to tell me every question they were asked during their interview. The same was true whether it was for medical school, a residency, or dental school. Sixty-one percent of the time, they were asked one of the three abovementioned questions—"winner, winner, chicken dinner." Thirty-seven percent of the time, they were asked two of the abovementioned questions—"the daily double." Twenty-one percent of the time, they had the trifecta and were asked all three of the abovementioned questions. That's why I call them "the big three."

I recommend that each student send me an e-mail of nine to twelve sentences with answers to each of those questions. We go back and forth by e-mail until both the student and I are happy with all three answers. No matter how many residency programs you apply to, questions one and two always stay the same. Question three is going to change depending on each and every residency program that you applied to, which means that you have to have individual responses and you need to get information from students you know who attended there or from the residency's website or hopefully from the fact that you did an elective rotation there. See chapter 11 on the Goldberg Method to perfect your responses.

Under no circumstances should you ever, ever infer that the city is desirable because of its climate or because you have always been a Browns fan or want to be near your parents. Never! Imagine a brilliant high-school student who loves science and loves teaching. This individual goes on to a great medical school and into a specialty residency and then gives up a higher income in the private sector to teach others and share his or her love of the specialty he or she has chosen. Imagine then how unbelievably rude and hurtful it would be to say, "Yes, I want to go to this school because I love the weather in South Florida." Or imagine if it was a professor at the University of Chicago and you said, "Oh, I've always been a White Sox fan." Or imagine if you were applying at Northwestern and said, "Oh, my parents live here, and I want to be near them." Never, never, never talk about anything except the advantages clinically and academically of the residency school you have chosen.

However, truth be told, when I attended a specific class on selecting your residency (many hospital-administration programs do have a residency), the professor directing the class was discussing in depth the merits of different types of residencies, such as working with a health plan, an insurance company, long-term care, a consulting firm, Certificate of Need Board, or a hospital. I remember saying, "I don't care where I go as long as it's Chicago."

The professor was outraged and said, "If Dr. J., PhD, the director of the program, heard what you said, you would be terminated from the graduate program."

I walked myself into Dr. J.'s office and said, "In our class for selecting a residency, I indicated to Dr. L. that I didn't care where I went or what I did as long as it was Chicago. Furthermore, Dr. L. said you would kick me out of the program if you knew I said this."

Fortunately for me, Dr. J. was a kind, gentle, helpful soul and said, "I think I have a friend at Lutheran General Hospital in Park Ridge. Is that near Chicago? Let me see if I can get you in there." He did, and I performed my administrative residency at Lutheran General Hospital.

Thank you, Dr. J.

Even though I am a hypocrite, please do what I say and not what I did, and don't say you want to go somewhere because of its location, weather, or baseball team.

Rehearse, Rehearse, Rehearse

After the student and I are both happy with what they've written, I ask them to start reading it every day, repeating each of the three answers to the three questions forty times a day for three days. Then I have them read it to me to make sure that the cadence, the timing, and the emphasis are perfect, and next I tell them to start memorizing them. After they memorize them, I go over it over and over and over and over and over again with them, and then when they're ready, we talk about handshakes and what to do with your hands. Again, please see chapter 11 on the Goldberg Method to perfect your responses.

Hands, Feet, and Eye Contact

Eye contact is extremely important, and if it's a one-on-one interview, your eyes should never leave the eyes of the person who's interviewing you. If there are multiple people interviewing you, you should look primarily at the person who asked the last question with direct eye contact and then glance every now and then at the other individuals.

I've noticed that there are typically two types of students. One is what I call roboto-man or roboto-woman, and the other is the passionate person with arms waving wildly. The goal is to combine the two. If your hands are always in your lap or at your side, that's not good. At least once or twice during the statements, you need to show some type of expression by your hands to emphasize your passion. No jittery feet. They need to be planted firmly without appearing jumpy.

The Six Sins of Interviewing

Don't ever, ever say "well," "uh," "and um," "actually," "well, actually," or "to tell the truth" at the beginning of a sentence. When you say "to tell you the truth," that means everything you have said before is a lie.

Rapid-Fire Questions

After "the big three" questions are memorized stone-cold, the other questions, which I call rapid-fire questions, should be reviewed for familiarity only.

What are your study habits?

How do you prepare for a test?

What is something you would change about yourself?

How would your best friend describe you?

If becoming a specialty doesn't work out, which other specialty would you pursue?

If you could spend time with anybody at any time in the past or in the future, whom would you meet with and why?

What is a current event that interests you, excluding Obamacare?

Describe to me what you are doing now aside from what your CV says.

How do you deal with stress?

What is your friend group at school like?

What are your hobbies?

What is the biggest challenge you have faced in your life?

If you are a physician, and a patient who had a scheduled routine exam or procedure tells you that they do not have money for the exam and then asks that you list it as an emergency and go through with the exam, what would you do?

How were you able to become involved in your research?

Describe how a patient's culture or religion can make it difficult for compliance or potentially be lost to follow-up. How would you handle it?

How has your experience allowed you to be more culturally sensitive?

Describe a case during rotations where you were very confident on a certain differential, but you missed something and you felt ashamed or humiliated by your preceptor. How did you handle it?

Describe a time when your organizational skills allowed you to make a better differential.

Describe a time when you had to stand up for something that was an unpopular decision among your peers.

Who is your role model and why?

You have a child with suspected meningitis, but the parents are refusing a spinal tap. What do you do?

What did you like about our program that made you want to apply here?

If you could do over something in your life, what would it be?

If a nurse called you in the middle of the night to come in, what personal quality about yourself would make the nurse glad that you were the doctor on call?

What do you feel are the biggest problems in medicine?

What do you think is the role of the nurse?

What do you think is the biggest problem faced by patients?

How do you work in group projects?

What if there was an aggressive group member or a group member who was not contributing?

What if someone told you that *you* weren't contributing to the group?

What would you say to your best friend if she asked you to look up her dad's medical records because he's in the hospital?

What would you do if you thought a med student falsified the lab results of a patient?

If you had a month to do whatever you wanted, what would it be?

What are your thoughts on euthanasia and assisted suicide?

Who had the biggest influence in your life and why?

Describe to me in the third person what you want me to write on *your* review sheet.

If you knew a patient had depression and could be suicidal, would you tell the patient that he or she had cancer?

If a person had a condition and declined a treatment that you know would help him or her, what should you do?

What Questions Do You Have?

You need to be prepared with at least two individual questions to ask the interviewers. Typically, they will ask at the end of the interview, "Do you have any questions of me?" They also might walk you from one building to another to take you to the next appointment, particularly if they like you. This is an opportunity to show how you stand out and have an intelligent question or two.

Your Handshake and Appearance

We then work with shaking hands, firm and dry whether a male or female. I hate to be old-fashioned, but appearance is important. Initial impressions are extremely important. Young people in your generation have the habit of starting each sentence with "well," as my generation used to start a sentence with "um" or "and um." It's important that you stick to the script, starting exactly where the script starts and not adding "well" in front of it.

Men should have neatly combed hair. Sorry, ponytails are out, and you should wear a white or blue oxford, preferably button-down shirt, conservative tie, and a blue sports coat and beige khakis or gray slacks, or better yet, a blue suit and appropriate shoes. Women, I'm sorry to be sexist, but please limit the jewelry, don't wear any perfume, and preferably dress in a white blouse, a nice navy or gray sports coat, a skirt or slacks, and appropriate shoes.

Many medical-school students ask me for advice regarding which residency they should pursue, both in terms of lifestyle and remuneration. I advise them that they are making a decision today that might not take effect for many years, and in the interim, the market can change.

In the early nineties, the government and many of the health-care pundits were predicting the growth in power and remuneration for primary-care physicians at the expense of subspecialists. I remember in 1994 and 1995, I received numerous calls from gastroenterologists, cardiologists, radiologists, and anesthesiologists who were willing to perform primary care in a clinic because they could not find a position in their chosen specialty. In the late nineties, and continuing through today, all of these specialties—gastroenterology, cardiology, radiology, pathology—have been in high demand and have very high rates of remuneration.

I have seen several medical students who could have selected any specialty they wanted and would most likely have been approved but who wanted to be pediatricians. This was their passion, this was what they felt would be rewarding in their lives, and they didn't care about lifestyle or financial remuneration. For those looking for more of a financial reward, it's hard to go wrong, at least for the foreseeable future, and based on past history, being an "-ologist"—that is, a radiologist, pathologist, anesthesiologist, dermatologist, otolaryngologist, ophthalmologist, hematologist, oncologist, or cardiologist.

Emergency-department medicine, both for adult and pediatrics, is currently very popular because the individual does not have to wear a beeper; does not have to worry about being a businessperson, unless directing the group; and can have a flexible schedule.

To quote the Beatles, "And in the end the love you take is equal to the love you make," or in this instance, the more you put into the process, the more you will get out of it.

An Example of a Great Personal Statement for a Residency

One of the experiences that led me to pursue a career as an obstetrician/gynecologist occurred while working on the medical mobile van parked at Sixteenth and Cicero. There was a woman who was recovering from a heroin addiction and was a victim of physical and sexual abuse. Cervical- and breast-cancer screening were far from her mind, as she was there for her Suboxone prescription and evaluation of a facial laceration. It is moments such as these that remind us of the unique problems that women face, and it is the importance of the bond between a female patient and her physician that propelled me into the field of OB/GYN.

OB/GYN is an ideal profession for me because it is a challenging field involving technical procedures, yet it also focuses on education, prevention, and a strong, long-lasting patient-physician relationship. This is one of the few specialties in which you can surgically treat a patient with cancer but also be on the forefront of cancer prevention in your outpatient clinic. This combination appeals to me, as I would be able to utilize all of my strengths. In addition, many medical specialties focus on pathological disease, whereas OB/GYN allows physicians to take part in an amazing physiologic process, pregnancy and childbirth. I am excited to be a part of such an important moment in my patients' lives, but I am also prepared to support my patients when the outcome is unexpected.

I have been drawn to women's health by the meaningful connections made during each patient encounter in clinics, in shelters, and throughout my third-year clerkships. While volunteering in the community during my preclinical years, I was disappointed to discover so many women who did not understand the importance of screening, had health misconceptions, or were afraid to seek care. I soon learned that by taking the time to educate patients in a clear and relevant manner, awareness of the importance of Pap smears, mammography, prenatal care, and proper use of contraception could be greatly enhanced. Education and prevention became the focus of my community outreach, and it was at this time that I founded Original Change Project, an organization with the aim to provide health education and referrals to free health and social services within the community.

I also found my niche in preventive medicine through my instruction in an adolescent sexual-health course, my research with the Chicago Breast Cancer Task Force, and my work on the medical mobile van. When I began my third-year clerkships, I discovered that misconceptions and a lack of information not only exist in the shelters and at health fairs at local food depositories but are widespread, afflicting people of all ages, ethnicities, education backgrounds, and socioeconomic levels. As a result of this, I have made it my goal to ensure that all my patients receive the proper education, support, screening, and health services needed to increase awareness of disease and enhance health and well-being within our community.

Throughout medical school I have displayed professionalism, dedication to academic achievement, and strength as a leader. More importantly, I have demonstrated a compassion and humanistic nature, which are valued qualities for an obstetrician/gynecologist to possess when dealing with such private medical concerns of patients. I am open-minded, compassionate, and dedicated to providing my patients with the best care possible. I have been honored by my classmates with induction into the Gold Humanism Honor Society for my dedication to service. While I deeply appreciate their recognition, the greatest honor is spending time to educate and support my patients. The phrase "patient advocate" has appeared several times on my evaluation. I take great pride in this, as I always do whatever is in my power to ensure that my patients are receiving the care that they deserve. I believe that the combination of compassion and determination for great patient care will serve me well as an obstetrician/gynecologist.

Looking back on that night on the mobile van, if I were her physician, I would be able to provide her with prenatal care, deliver her children, provide appropriate screening, and intervene surgically if necessary. Most importantly, I would be able to support her through her drug rehabilitation and provide her with every resource possible to better her personal and social situation. It is the diversity of this specialty and the unique nature of the patient population and medical concerns that have influenced me to enter the field of OB/GYN. When evaluating my goals as a physician along with my experiences, strengths, and attributes, I believe that I could make a valuable contribution to the residency program and the medical field, merging all of my strengths in order to provide the best care possible to my patients.

Editorial comment: I made a few grammatical changes only.

Preparing for the Residency Interview
(Examples from medical school students.)

Student #1

Tell me about yourself.

I was born in Scotland. My dad's training had us move around a lot, and I spent time in the United Kingdom, Saudi Arabia, and Canada before moving to the United States. I have been living around Chicago for some time now, excluding the four years I spent in college, when I went to the University of Illinois at Urbana-Champaign and studied finance. I have an older sister who's a marketing professional and a younger brother in high school. When I'm not at school, I am pretty religious about going to the gym, and I enjoy golfing. My biggest passion outside of medicine is food. I love exploring new cuisines in Chicago, and the food scene is usually the first thing I check out in a new city.

Why do you want to be a radiologist?

My interest in radiology developed during anatomy class my first year. At the time I really enjoyed learning anatomy and correlating it with plain films and CTs. After that I spent some time with radiologists at Loyola and grew fascinated with their utilization of technology and their fluency in the diagnosis and treatment of pathology from head to toe. I liked that when radiologists go over a study, they more or less start out with a blank slate. Although they may have some history, once they open up a study, they can find just about anything, and they have to go back and put together a diagnosis, or identify multiple problems, almost like a puzzle. But what makes radiology truly meaningful to me is what I saw during my third year when I rotated through all my clerkships and saw how all of these clinicians, in vastly different fields, based their care on the interpretations and recommendations given by radiologists. Being able to utilize such a large amount of knowledge to partake in the care of such a wide variety of patients is what brings me to the field.

Why do you want to go to _____?

For academic programs:

Part of the reason I like radiology is because of how innovative the field is. Continuous research is being done, and advancements are being made at the physics level, in designing new equipment and developing new indications and studies with the available technology. With so much innovation going on, I want to join an academic program so that I can find my own area of interest and work alongside distinguished mentors to make my own contributions to the field while in residency. A few particular things I like about this program are...[will fill in once I know where I will be interviewing.]

For community programs:

Part of the reason I like radiology is how fluent radiologists are in illnesses from head to toe. In the future I want to be a radiologist who can interpret any study, perform a wide array of radiologic procedures, and partake in the care of patients across all services in the hospital and outpatient clinics. With this goal in mind, I want to come to a community program where I will be able to get ample hands-on experience alongside great teachers so that I can leave residency with the knowledge and confidence to be an all-encompassing asset at my future hospital. When I was selecting programs to apply to, I wasn't looking for flashy names or fancy cities but rather programs that would provide me with the ample training needed to be a competent radiologist. A few specific things I like about this program are…[will fill in once I know where I will be interviewing.]

Comment: Very good. This person knew he wanted to be a radiologist before medical school, so he took radiology electives and participated in radiology research.

Student #2

Tell me about yourself.

I have always been interested in science and helping people. I appreciate the satisfaction I gain from helping others and the relationships I am able to develop. For six years I worked as a medical assistant and transportation manager for a medical practice. I enjoyed medical school and loved my clinical rotations. I work hard at everything I do. In my spare time, I play numerous sports, teach and learn dance, and participate in filmmaking.

Why do you want to be an internist?

The internist is the first entry point for many patients into the health-care system and directs their care by diagnosis and treatment. If more analysis or treatment is required, the internist decides which specialists can help provide the appropriate diagnosis and treatment. Preventative care and patient education are important roles for the internist, and I want to positively impact the lives of my patients with continuity of care. My preceptors in internal medicine were respectable, intelligent, hardworking, and passionate physicians. They inspire me, and I want to be a great physician like them.

Why do you want to do your family-medicine residency at Susquehanna Health Williamsport?

I am aware that you treat all of your staff like family. Each individual is respected and supported in a truly collegial environment. Your program emphasizes education and clinical skills as well.

I believe these components are essential for a person to thrive and become the best doctor he is capable of being. Your program offers the perfect opportunity to start a life that balances medicine, family, and other passions. Your family-centered model of patient care has great appeal to me. I not only want to train at your hospital but also want to contribute to your program and community.

Why do you want to do your internal-medicine residency at SIU Springfield?

Your program is a great match for me. At the end of my three years of training in internal medicine, I want to be the most complete physician possible. I think you can make that possible with your highly qualified teaching staff, focus on educational priority and resident well-being, and prestigious programs like your cardiac-care and fellowship opportunities. I am intrigued by your large and diverse patient population, as I want to be exposed to the entire continuum of disease and behavioral sciences. I can see myself flourishing at your program and would be honored to be a valuable and contributing member to SIU Springfield.

Why do you want to do your family-medicine residency at the University of Toledo program?

I would be grateful if your program would allow me to train along the entire continuum of care. You train your residence in university and community hospital settings, clinics, and even your patient-centered medical home (PCMH). Preventative and continuous care are most important for me to be a successful primary-care physician. I want to train in a high-quality teaching environment like yours, and I am also impressed with your geriatric fellowship program at Saint Luke's Hospital. I believe you can make me a competent and caring primary-care physician who will contribute to your program and community.

Why do you want to do your internal-medicine residency at Nassau University?

I would be so excited to participate in your comprehensive training program. I want to be competent in all areas of medicine as a primary-care physician. I believe you have a high-quality educational environment as your teams range from attendings to medical students. Your conference and lecture schedule is a great way to learn and has great appeal to me. Your program contains every characteristic I am looking for in residency. I think you are a great match for me, and I would contribute to your program and community.

Student #3

Tell me about yourself.

Starting in high school, I worked at a pediatric-OB/GYN practice, first as medical assistant and then at the administrative level. I enjoyed the sciences and working with patients, and I solidified my desire to become a physician. Gaining experience through my time at Loyola University Chicago and at Caribbean for medical school, I valued the hard work that was in everything I did. I was very active in health-related organizations and traveled to many countries developing health programs and working in mobile clinics. I learned from physicians and others how to become a leader around campus among other future physicians. I was very involved in many organizations creating a strong sense of global health awareness and engaging students to have more active roles as future providers of health care. In medical school I continued to grow as a leader by starting a trend of community health fairs that now run every semester. During rotations, I continued to learn from physicians as role models and was recognized as an honor student. I collaborated well with the attending and team of medical students while also helping to train the newer medical students.

Why do you want to be an OB/GYN?

My experiences through the years have strengthened my desire to be an OB/GYN. After each international trip, I knew I wanted to return as a physician to provide health care to women in underserved areas. Through medical-school rotations, I observed attendings provide an environment of comfort, understanding, and clinical skills on a one-on-one level. Being an OB/GYN will allow me to use all of my strengths in a versatile way in the many roles I have had in the health-care field. Nothing has been more exciting to me than the responsibilities as an OB/GYN. The physiological changes of a woman's body are fascinating. With a warm smile and full attention, I want to be the kind of OB/GYN that is always available to care for a woman's needs at any stage in her life.

Why do you want to do your OB/GYN residency at Queens Hospital Center?

I have a strong history of working in underserved populations, and I wish to work in a residency program that is dedicated to working in underserved communities and promotes diversity, accessibility, and quality of care to everyone regardless of background. As an enthusiastic young future OB/GYN, I am committed to hard work and want to work in a community hospital where I will be able to receive hands-on experience so I can complete the residency with the knowledge and confidence to be an excellent OB/GYN. Among the components I like about this program at Queens Hospital Center are the communities that you serve. I also believe in your mission to serve "multicultural and ethnically diverse patient populations." I look forward to this opportunity to be a contributor to this model, and I value the hospital's development of primary-care and specialty services focusing on training OB/GYN residents to be "primary care providers in the new healthcare environment" for women.

Student #4

Why do you want to be a family-medicine doctor?

I have always worked in primary-care settings. As a medical assistant, I learned to treat everyone from neonates to their grandparents in one clinic. We were able to focus on methods of treatment while also stressing the importance of preventative care. After being promoted to the administrative level, I developed a program for obese teenage patients to learn about healthy living through nutrition and personal trainers. My experiences through medical school have strengthened my desire to be a family-medicine doctor. In every experience I have had, I have watched as family practitioners provided comprehensive care to the entire community through patience and diligence. This method of holistic medicine was consistent throughout my training in clinical rotations, as my family-medicine attendings were all enthusiastic doctors offering various options of treatment and preventative care. They were able to focus not just on the disease but environment and the family as a whole.

Why do you want to do your family-medicine residence at Presence Saints Mary and Elizabeth Medical Center?

I have a strong history of working in underserved populations with the career goal to work in a residency program that is dedicated to working in underserved communities and promotes diversity, accessibility, and quality of care to everyone regardless of background. As an enthusiastic young future family physician, I am committed to hard work and want to work in a community hospital where I will be able to receive hands-on experience so I can complete the residency with the knowledge and confidence to be an excellent physician. Among the components I like about the program at Presence Saints Mary and Elizabeth Medical Center is the pride you have in serving your community. As a hallmark of your facility, you have provided outstanding, compassionate medical services in a patient- and family-centered environment. As a Chicago native, I look forward to this opportunity to be a contributor to this model, and I value the program's dedication to providing substantial training in medicine, critical care, OB, and pediatrics/neonatology.

SO, YOU
WANT TO BE
A PHYSICIAN

C H A P T E R   1 8

COULD THE PRINCIPLES IN THIS BOOK APPLY TO PREPARING FOR INTERVIEWS FOR OTHER POSITIONS?

Yes, particularly the questions "Tell me about yourself" and "Why would you like to work at this organization?" This would involve the same type of dedication to learning about your potential employer but should also include what you can do for the employer.

Good preparation equals good luck.

CHAPTER 19

WHAT IF YOU DON'T GET IN?

There are several programs that offer postgraduate, premedical education degrees, such as a master of science in biology/chemistry at Loyola, Northwestern, Midwest University, Rosalind Franklin, or Bennington College in Vermont. I am sure that there are many others. The Bennington College program offers two courses in biology and chemistry over ten months, followed by two months preparing for the MCATs. They allegedly have a high medical-school acceptance rate. Their phone number is 802-442-5401, and the website for their program is http://www.bennington.edu/academics/graduate-postbac-programs/postbaccalaureate-premedical-program.

Johns Hopkins University also has a postbaccalaureate premedical program. Their telephone number is 410-516-7748. Their website is http://krieger.jhu.edu/postbac.

Other options include getting new experiences—for example, being a scribe in an emergency department or performing research—or if it was the MCATs that hurt you, receiving tutoring or retaking the Kaplan course.

Or if you didn't take a Kaplan course before, take one now.

My personal experience is that Northwestern, Loyola, Midwest University, and Rosalind Franklin have never admitted a master's student I have known. I have known a student who attended Bennington College in Vermont who was accepted into medical school.

CHAPTER 20
OTHER OPTIONS

When students ask me about being a doctor of osteopath or going to a foreign medical school, I respond with the following questions.

"Do you know what they call an individual who finishes Harvard Medical School first in his or her class?"

Response: "Doctor."

"Do you know what they call the individual who finished last in his or her medical-school class at Guadalajara?"

Response: "Doctor."

"Do you know what Medicare pays a primary-care physician from Harvard who finished first in his or her class for a routine visit?"

Response: "The same that they pay a primary-care physician who finished last in his or her class at Guadalajara."

I don't personally find any difference between MDs and DOs, although some people might. Quite frankly, from my experience, it's just about as difficult to get into a DO school as an MD school.

What I have learned from students that applied to a DO school, and from an osteopathic physician on my medical staff who serves as an interviewer for one of the DO medical schools, is that DO schools look very favorably on those applicants who have only applied to DO schools. In other words, if you are applying to DO schools as a backup, they would take this as a negative.

On the other hand, if you applied to all DO schools in different states, they would see that as a positive. Additionally, the two students that I coached who were accepted to DO schools both were thoroughly familiar with the history and philosophy of osteopathic medicine and were both passionate about it, and I am confident this was a very significant advantage to them in their acceptance.

Class rank and medical school can have an impact on which residencies you can be accepted in to, but your Step I and Step II board scores are the most important factor in the residencies you can be accepted in to.

Obviously, the foreign medical schools in my day were in Mexico, typically Guadalajara, but now there is a plethora of medical schools in the Caribbean, India, and Europe, which have easier criteria than American schools. An online search can quickly help find the right fit, but I have listed a few links below that might prove useful.

Mexico: http://www.iime.org/database/northam/mexico.htm
Caribbean: http://en.wikipedia.org/wiki/List_of_medical_schools_in_the_Caribbean
India: http://en.wikipedia.org/wiki/Medical_Schools_in_India
Europe: http://en.wikipedia.org/wiki/List_of_medical_schools_in_Europe

CHAPTER 21

OTHER HEALTH CARE-RELATED FIELDS

Much to my surprise, one student called me and asked if he could go through the interview coaching process to become a physician assistant. The individual had a very decent grade point average (a 3.6 at Duke) and had an acceptable but not great score on the MCATs (a twenty-eight). He interviewed very well. I asked him why he didn't want to go to medical school, and he indicated that he had given a great deal of thought to this and that if he did become a physician, he would most likely be a pediatrician. For approximately one-quarter of the time in school, he would make almost as much being a physician assistant as a pediatrician, and he wouldn't have to carry a beeper or be a business-man. Additionally, because he already had an undergraduate degree, he could complete the program in two years. There are alternatives to being a physician, such as nurse practitioner, physician assistant, certified nurse midwife, and certified nurse anesthetist.

I would just highly recommend you don't become a hospital administrator, unless you're into sadomasochism.

SO, YOU
WANT TO BE
A PHYSICIAN

CHAPTER 22
TESTIMONIALS

In the years I had been advising medical-school applicants before I wrote the book, I had asked only one thing in return: that they write back to me and tell me about their trials, tribulations, and experiences in the application and—hopefully—acceptance process.

This chapter is a compilation of testimonials I have received over twelve years of coaching.

Edward Goldberg gives you the pieces needed to get into medical school. You just have to put them together. This book is methodical and thoughtful, and I was surprised that someone could take such a dull and mechanical subject and turn it into such a fun, practical, and inspiring read. This book will help you get into medical school, or any healthcare profession you may be considering, including veterinary medicine, advance practice nursing, dentistry and so on.

—Robin Bruscato

———

Mr. Goldberg is an incredible coach and mentor. I don't think I'd be where I am now—at my first choice medical school—without his help guiding me through the medical school application process. *So You Want to Be a Physician* is an excellent resource that outlines his recommendations for the various aspects of being a successful applicant. As a first time applicant who knew I would make a kind, motivated, and skilled physician, I wanted guidance from someone knowledgeable, so I would have the best possible chance of achieving my dreams of helping to improve people's lives. Mr. Goldberg helped me attain the first major step in that goal: getting accepted into medical school. He assisted me with my personal statement, interviewing skills, letters of update, and everything in between. I am extremely grateful for all of his help, and I couldn't imagine anyone better for the task.

—Rita

———

Even if you've broken the curve in organic chemistry, volunteered every weekend since you were in kindergarten, and gotten one better than a perfect score on the MCAT, the medical school application process can seem daunting. Goldberg takes the fear and mystery away from the process and puts you on the path taken by hundreds of successful applicants.

Edward Goldberg and "So, You Want to Be a Physician" were fundamental to my medical school application and interview process. This book helped me with everything from school selection to essay writing and ultimately preparing for the interview. Thanks to this book, I got into medical school on my first try and saved thousands of dollars that would have been spent on a failed admissions attempt.

Unlike other coaches that emphasize changing things that simply cannot be changed, Mr. Goldberg explains how to put your best foot forward and show the admissions committee why they need you at their school. Goldberg helps you find your story and express it through your experiences in a way admissions staff will actually want to read. Furthermore, thanks to *So, You Want to Be a Physician*, I felt comfortable walking into the interview because I understood my own strengths and weaknesses in a way I could clearly express.

I'm now in my first semester at a school I love, and I've been able to find a research position thanks to the same techniques Goldberg taught me for the admissions process. This book is a must read for anyone who wants to be a physician!!!

—Andy

———

I entered the interviewing process for Internal Medicine residency without a firm grasp on how to conduct myself in the "real world." I did not have a complete understanding of how most processes worked. Mr. Goldberg's comprehensive program included an easy-to-read book and one-on-one coaching sessions. More importantly, he genuinely cared about my success. He was able to fine tune all of my best qualities and I became much more confident in myself. I became an outstanding candidate and I was accepted at my residency of choice. I continue to stand out and I am grateful for Mr. Goldberg's support and guidance throughout my journey.

—Nath

———

This book mapped out all the variables and appropriate steps for my journey to enter medical school. It was extremely helpful as entering medical school is a difficult feat to say the least. I was able to walk into my interview both extremely confident and at a very low level of stress. Highly recommended for anyone thinking of pursuing a career in medicine.

—Eric

———

Mr. Goldberg's book, personal statement revisions, and coaching helped me during residency interviews become a very confident and desirable applicant. He was able to help me express myself in a thoughtful and exciting manner which made my interviews and personal statement exhibit my true desires for pursuing a career in medicine. I am grateful for the one-on-one coaching he was able to provide and the outcome of landing me in my top choice of residency program.

—Tana

———

Mr. Goldberg's coaching allowed me to effectively and eloquently share my unique story with medical schools during the interview process. Besides sharing his invaluable advice, he took interest in me as a person and helped me feel confident going into interviews.

—Kelly

———

If only our child had known Mr. Goldberg during college freshman year, a lot of misdirected efforts in the premed college years would have been avoided, and the child's academic preparation and ECs would have been better aligned with the med school application. Mr. Goldberg is very knowledgeable about the medical school requirements, his advice is spot on and he is completely dedicated to the success of his students. When our child was not successful in the first attempt, he himself initiated coaching in the next go-around with no additional charge.

With the advent of MMI at more medical schools, he also worked with our child on how to prepare for MMI in addition to the traditional interview process. He is very patient in working with strong-willed students like ours. We recommend him without any reservation.

—Ram

———

I have been a general Internist for over thirty-five years, and had the pleasure of working with Edward Goldberg for eighteen of those years when he served as CEO of St. Alexius Medical Center.

I retired about eighteen months after he did, but he was probably one of twenty-five administrators who I worked with throughout my career. Mr. Goldberg was passionate about being physician and employee-friendly in everything he did.

Mr. Goldberg was always the first one in and the last one out, and many times he would be coaching aspiring Medical School students after hours. He had an interesting teaching manner, in which he would work with the students on several interview questions that prior students had been asked, and have them write a script that they felt comfortable with, and then practice it, including eye contact and posture. As I used to walk by his office on my way home, I saw how much he cared for his students' success, the same as he did his employees and physicians. Many of his students were sons or daughters of physicians on the medical staff or employees of the hospital.

After I retired, I bought a copy of the book, and could actually hear Mr. Goldberg's voice through the pages. Mr. Goldberg sheds light on many of the issues facing physicians, but most importantly focuses on those students in High School or college who have a good shot at getting into Medical School, and then making sure they have the best possible personal statement and interview that shows the Medical School the very best components the applicants have to offer.

I would highly recommend this to anyone considering applying to any of the healthcare professions.

—Dr. Robert Dick

———

Achieving one's lifelong career goals can be difficult enough without the anxiety generated by worrying if you are on the right path or by trying to navigate the complexities of a professional school admissions process. In this easily readable book Edward Goldberg draws on his nearly forty years of experience in healthcare to provide a brief but thorough reference for those interested in not only becoming a physician but also for those interested in many of the other career opportunities available in the healthcare fields.

The advice in this book comes from an individual who knows whereof he speaks. In his vast experience as a hospital administrator Mr. Goldberg has befriended health professionals at all levels. He has generously given personal and professional advice to doctors, nurses and hospital employees. It is a very natural transition for him to extend his observations and expertise to those wishing to enter healthcare fields.

Most importantly Mr. Goldberg has kept pace with the myriad changes that have affected healthcare training as well as the delivery of services. His broad view of current trends in education, professional opportunity, subspecialization, finance, healthcare policy and the personal demands of each field can help students maximize their ability to define and ultimately achieve their career goals.

This book belongs in the library of every high school or college guidance counselor as well as on the shelf of those preparing for a career as a medical professional.

—Allen E. Saxon, MD

———

A must read book!

After reading Ed Goldberg's book, I was struck by the very specific suggestions he offered to help students understand and follow the specific process they need to follow to get into med school.

However, Ed goes one step further, emphasizing the importance of the student's personal presentation during the interview as well as his ability to communicate his achievements and accomplishments. A knockout combination!

Ed Goldberg is uniquely qualified to tutor aspiring medical students, having worked in many diverse medical situations. He is highly knowledgeable, articulate and has a keen, irrepressible sense of humor. He is generous in sharing his experiences and has had a great deal of success in preparing students for a successful future.

—Doris Nixon

———

As an internist practicing for thirty-three years, I have four children all coached by Mr. Goldberg for their personal statements, applications and interviews. My oldest son is beginning his fourth year of his ENT residency program, my second son is in his third year of medical school and my other two children are starting medical school in the fall. Mr. Goldberg's assistance has been invaluable. His no-nonsense, sometimes brutally honest approach, and his philosophy of "practice, practice, practice" ensures that the student has the very best opportunity to present to the medical school who he/she really is. If you are serious about becoming a doctor, you should buy Mr. Goldberg's book and utilize his coaching services.

—Warren Pierce, MD

———

Simply put, Mr. Goldberg's book and coaching services assisted me in gaining acceptance into medical school. I am currently a second year medical student attending the medical school of my choice, in large part due to Mr. Goldberg's book and coaching services!

I purchased and referenced Mr. Goldberg's book extensively during the medical school application process. During that process, I contacted Mr. Goldberg, seeking advice on my application and to inquire about his coaching services. I was hesitant to spend money on coaching services, but I was so impressed by the clarity gained from Mr. Goldberg's book and advice that I gave it a go. I am very thankful I did as the results speak for themselves…I applied to thirteen medical schools. I received interview invitations to eleven of the thirteen and was accepted at all the schools I scheduled interviews with. I am absolutely confident that Mr. Goldberg's book and coaching services were instrumental in my success!

Perhaps the greatest advantage Mr. Goldberg offers is his ability to clearly see how medical schools will view you as an applicant. His experience allows him to view applications and applicants through the same lens as medical school admissions committees. This removes the mystery behind gaining acceptance into medical school and is invaluable! He has an uncanny method of discovering application mistakes and, as exemplified in my application, he knows exactly how to fix them!

As I look to the future, I plan to again seek Mr. Goldberg's services and advice as I prepare for acceptance into residency programs. Like me, I believe you will find great success utilizing Mr. Goldberg's book and coaching services!

—Shawn

———

Mr. Goldberg is a miracle worker in transforming inexperienced students into confident speakers. I have seen his magical power work for my older brother and then two years later, he also helped me get accepted into a medical program by sharpening my interviewing skill. My parents were so impressed by him that after my brother's acceptance into a medical program, they sent him a gift basket and were beside themselves with gratitude. Mr. Goldberg genuinely cares about his students and not just as a statistical case. He would take the time to communicate with parents as needed about the student's progress and will go above and beyond the call of duty to prepare the student by the deadline. He's an ACE and I would have him on my team any day!!!

—Kevin

———

As a BA/MD applicant, I had little experience with interviews and thus was very nervous about my prospects. However, after working with Mr. Goldberg through a series of mock interviews and running my essays by him, I was given the confidence I needed to approach the application process with eagerness as opposed to a more reticent disposition. My gratitude toward Mr. Goldberg and his help is endless. In fact, I truly believe that had it not been for Mr. Goldberg's help, I would not have received as many BA/MD program acceptances as I did. I'm definitely hoping to work with him again when it comes time to apply for residency, and recommend his services to anyone considering a career in healthcare.

—Shani Chibber

———

I wanted to let you know that I matched at UIC for radiology. I was really excited to find this out a couple weeks ago. I meant to tell you earlier, but believe it or not, school has gotten much busier after Match Day rather than the smooth sailing till graduation I was hoping for. Thank you once again for all your interview and personal statement help. I felt pretty confident that I nailed my interviews. I look forward to future interactions and conversations with you.

—Senthil Gunasekaran

———

My conversations with Mr. Goldberg completely changed my outlook on interviewing. Previous to our first meeting, I assumed my natural conversational abilities would carry me through a dental school interview. When I sat down with Mr. Goldberg, he made me realize I was stumbling through my words while talking about my own life experiences. In just a few days, I was completely prepared to discuss the important parts of my pre-dental life. Additionally, Mr.

Goldberg helped me improve my speaking skills and made sure I would be dressed to impress. I felt very confident and prepared for my interview. I am so thankful for the opportunity to be mentored by Mr. Goldberg. He has incredible insight into what it takes to ace an interview. Thank you again Mr. Goldberg!

—Colleen McShane

Meeting with Mr. Goldberg helped me tremendously in the interview process. After meeting with him, I felt that I had sharpened my ability to speak clearly and professionally while still conveying my personality and values. Although I was not sure what questions would be asked on interview day, I was more prepared to answer unexpected questions. I very much appreciate his help and would recommend interview training/practice to anyone working toward a career in medicine.

—Chelsey McShane

Hi! I just wanted to let you know that I was accepted to UIC. I just found out this weekend. I am very excited about it. I had an interview at Washington University in St. Louis two weeks ago, which went well. Thank you so much!

—Jori Sheade

I hope you are doing well! Senior year is coming to an end for me, and I am pleased to tell you that I will be attending UIC's GPPA Medical Program. I would like to thank you again for helping me during this application process. Your interview method and book were all extremely helpful!

—Carolyn Cao

I wanted to thank you again for helping me during the interviewing process. By practicing interview questions and skills with you, I felt more confident and comfortable during my own interviews, especially when challenging questions arose. I also learned appropriate etiquette and manners to use during the interview. Multiple interviewers commended me on my interview skills, and I have you to thank for that.

—Elie Schwartz

My name is James B. McShane, and I am a dentist on staff at Alexian Brothers Hospital. I have known Mr. Edward Goldberg since my four children were small. They are now in their late teens and early twenties and have begun to benefit from a rare and valuable talent Mr. Goldberg possesses, the ability to teach others how to conduct themselves during interviews for admission to professional schools.

Mr. Goldberg, president and CEO of St. Alexius Medical Center, once told me that he put a high value on young people and took great pride in helping deserving students achieve their dreams. He mentioned that so as not to be overwhelmed, he limited this coaching service to the children of the medical staff at St. Alexius and employees. This did not surprise me as Mr. Goldberg has a longstanding reputation for being physician- and employee-friendly. In 2010 my oldest child was granted several interviews for admission to dental schools. She had nice credentials but was uncertain about her interview skills. I met personally with Mr. Goldberg and asked him if he would help her. He not only agreed but invited me to sit out of sight and within earshot so I could get a feel for his technique and appreciate my daughter's improve-ment. The results were amazing. After a few rather intense sessions, she not only knew what was important to say but realized the significance of posture, eye contact, attire, and much more. About a month later, my second daughter was granted an interview for medical school. Mr. Goldberg generously afforded her the same attention. As you might guess, this story has a happy ending, as both my girls are currently concluding their first years of dental and medical school respectively.

Since then I have referred three more hopefuls to Mr. Goldberg. Interestingly, one had fine credentials but did not survive the interview phase of her application process to medical school two years earlier. Another was applying to a physician-assistant program, and the most recent was attempting to gain admission to veterinary school. All three have been admitted, and it is my belief that their improved interview skills were a significant factor in their success. I also have two sons, both of which are interested in dentistry, and if they are fortunate enough to be granted interviews, you can be sure I will ask Mr. Goldberg to help them. I know he will help with any residency interviews as well.

The competition for seats in professional schools today is as fierce as it ever has been. Obviously, all these applicants had outstanding credentials to be granted interviews, but the odds are still tough at that point. Edward Goldberg's advice and encouragement have proven invaluable time after time, and I would like to personally thank him for his time and mostly for his concern for the future of medicine in our country.

—James B. McShane, DDS

Before I met Mr. Goldberg, I considered myself a naturally strong interviewer and public speaker. When I was rejected from my first medical school interview on my second attempt to pursue medicine, all of my confidence in interviewing was brought into question. It was a defeating feeling to realize my prior interviewing strategy was not effective; I knew I needed help. Mr. Goldberg helped me revise my strategy, keep some of my strengths, and work on new strengths.

When we first met in January 2011, he introduced new interviewing techniques that I had never considered before. At first, I was reluctant to introduce changes. Learning to prepare scripts for interview questions felt unnatural to me. When I overcame my stubbornness and used his method, they were effective and granted me two school acceptances. I do not intend to revert to my old habits ever again; I learned my lesson.

Mr. Goldberg helped me realize that I was coming across as an arrogant applicant with an attitude in my medical school interviews, which was not a true representation of my character. It certainly was not how I wanted to be remembered by interviewers. Mr. Goldberg set me straight in my mentality and taught me a valuable lesson about humility. I then accepted that I did not know it all and I was certainly not an expert. I was still a student when it came to interviewing, which was the first lesson I needed to learn. His teachings were the reality check I needed to pinpoint exactly why I wanted to pursue medicine, how to approach an interview, and how I wanted to present myself.

When interviewing with Mr. Goldberg, I was challenged to maintain a balance of confidence and humility. Even under pressure, I learned how to speak articulately and concisely. I knew I was a difficult student, set in my ways, and Mr. Goldberg continued to meet with me time after time. I could tell he was truly dedicated to help me the best that he could.

I was able to apply my new "Goldberg" interviewing skills in three medical school interviews. I was waitlisted at one school and accepted into the other two schools. I believe those acceptances were due to his contributions in molding me into a stronger interviewer. I was able to offer my best self in the interviews through my words, body language, and general presentation. I intend to carry his teachings with me in future interviews for residency and beyond. This experience was a career-changing lesson, and I am eternally grateful.

—Joyce Jhang

I entered medical school immediately following my undergraduate education. As a result, I'd never had an interview for anything more than a part-time job. Although I had good grades, extracurricular activities, and research, I was inexperienced at interviewing. Given the importance of the interview in medical school admissions, I turned to Mr. Goldberg for help. With his help, I learned to smoothly integrate my strengths, such as my research experience, when responding to questions. In addition, he taught me important skills that can apply to all interviews and will undoubtedly help me in the future. Because of the help of Mr. Goldberg, I was calm and confident during my medical school interviews, and was successful in receiving an acceptance.

—Josh Newman

I believe that my acceptance into medical school was due, in large part, to the mentoring I received from Mr. Goldberg. Having the academic credentials to qualify for med school is just the starting point of a long, arduous process. Having no physicians in the family, I had no idea what to expect from the application process, which resulted in a number of esteem-crushing rejections. A family friend introduced me to Mr. Goldberg, who understood what I was going through, and although we had never met before, he agreed to help me achieve my dream.

As the president/CEO of a hospital, his candid advice and familiarity with the expectations of medical school admission was invaluable. His interviewing technique advice helped me ace my third and last interview with the University of Miami-Miller School of Medicine, where I was eventually accepted. This is why I believe strongly in Mr. Goldberg's mentorship. I went on the have a wonderful four-year experience at UM and matched at my first choice of residency programs, Northwestern Memorial Hospital in Chicago, where I will start in June 2012. Thank you to Mr. Goldberg for helping me achieve my goal.

—Veronica Penyak

I was aspiring to gain admission to a competitive direct admission medical program from high school. With the help of Mr. Goldberg, I was able to achieve my goal. He gives individual training for interviews, and brought out the best in me. He taught me how to highlight my abilities, spirit, and commitment to medicine at a conversational, yet professional, level.

—Toral Vaidya

During my studies at the Medical College at Rush University, I had heard from others about Mr. Goldberg's superior coaching skills. So when the time came for me to apply for a residency in obstetrics, I felt confident that he was the right person to approach to help strengthen my application in the competitive rush for securing a residency. My instincts were spot on, and his excellent insight into the medical field and honest advice allowed me to hone in on the most important details to emphasize in my residency application personal statement.

After making the changes to the personal statement that Mr. Goldberg and I originally discussed, I continued to be impressed by his interest and commitment in assisting me with further refinement to my writing in subsequent drafts. While working with Mr. Goldberg, I found him to be kind, professional, and very effective. I feel his coaching played a big part in my success in gaining the residency I'd always hoped for, and I am grateful for his guidance. I would absolutely recommend Mr. Goldberg's tutoring to all medical school applicants, and those who are seeking their ideal residency match.

—Tara Usakoski

I met Mr. Goldberg at St. Alexius Hospital when I was there to implement the scribe program. He was very welcoming and enthusiastic about my ambition of becoming a physician. Aside from talking about medicine, which he is vastly passionate about, he is definitely someone who can hold a conversation with you about anything, including the color blue! His optimistic attitude and motivation to succeed influenced me to reach for the stars. Once I told him about applying to medical school I saw his desire to help me achieve the best and he offered to assist me with my essay writing. His advice on polishing my essay was immensely helpful. Furthermore, he gave me a different perspective on how to write my essays, and how to highlight my accomplishments without having to sound conceited. He has been a great influence on my acceptance into medical school, and I have been honored to have had the privilege of knowing him. He is definitely a great resource and played a strong force in my journey of becoming a physician.

—Afsha Rais

I was a special case, and probably a challenge, for Mr. Goldberg. I was offered his services late in the game. I had already taken the MCAT, written the personal statement and entrance essays, received letters of recommendation, and sent out applications to medical schools. In fact, by the time I started to converse with him, I had already scheduled two of my interviews. We had to act fast to perfect my presentation and my dialogue, involving writing out the answers to the three most frequently asked questions. In a matter of one afternoon, we went from the initial flawed version to a product that I liked and that Mr. Goldberg agreed was good. Although only one of the questions came up, I was prepared to answer the question, although it was asked in such a way that I could not use the script, it still allowed me to make sure to mention all of the key points.

I attended undergraduate school far away and I could not easily come home, so I was forced to meet him the morning of the day I was going to travel to Arizona for my interview. Although not the most convenient circumstances, I am glad that I was able to meet him in person. It was ironic that all of the areas I felt I was weaker in (eye contact, fluid speaking in interviews, etc.), Mr. Goldberg said I did nearly perfectly and the areas that I didn't think I needed to work on were the ones he said I needed to fix. He told me that my presence was among the best of all whom he had helped, which made me feel significantly more confident. That is the most important thing that I have taken from all of his assistance; the boost in confidence and the advice to change what was weak.

Although I did not get accepted to the school that he helped me with, I did get accepted into the school with the later interview date. I took what Mr. Goldberg told me as well as my experience with the first school and was able to apply it for the second one. I have since referred a couple people to his book, including a fellow student and my pre-medical adviser, who said she would research it and possibly use it for future students. I honestly wish I could have obtained his assistance a year or two earlier to benefit from all of the other information on MCAT preparation, mission statement critiques, and undergraduate advice, but in the end, I got into my dream medical school, so I am thankful for the assistance I received.

—Ashton Brunn

———

I wanted to let you know that I was accepted into the GPPA Program, and I would like to thank you for your help and time commitment as I was preparing for the interview. I was also accepted into the six-year BA/MD program at the University of Missouri—Kansas City, and I was able to translate some of the skills from our practice sessions to the interviews for that medical school as well. Again, thank you for all of your help; I really appreciate it!

—Eddy Nabrinsky

———

I cannot thank Mr. Goldberg enough for his help and knowledge in the application process to dental school. His professionalism demonstrates a genuine care and respect for anyone who walks through his door. While working with Mr. Goldberg, we focused on the interview process. He taught me professional and interview etiquette, and how to present myself in the best light. We collectively discussed my experience and volunteer work, and how to effectively communicate my passion for dentistry. He taught me what to emphasize during the interview and how to express it. Working with Mr. Goldberg was very beneficial in my preparation for interviews; I felt very prepared on the interview day. His advice and generosity met and exceeded my expectations. I highly recommend him to anyone who is looking to enter professional school.

—Elyse Zarek

———

When I first corresponded with Mr. Goldberg about interview tutoring, he asked me the question I had been dreading to answer: Why do you want to be a doctor? Don't get me wrong—being a physician will be a wonderful and fulfilling profession for me. However, the "why" had been very difficult for me to put into words. Not until I met with Mr. Goldberg was I able to verbalize my feelings toward the medical profession. Through collaborative discussion, a *lot* of drafts, and even more editing, I was able to really pinpoint what it was about being a doctor that made it the profession I needed to follow. Because of Mr. Goldberg's mentoring, I was successful during this application cycle, receiving invitations to four of the five medical schools with whom I interviewed.

—Tovah Schwartz

———

My interactions with Mr. Goldberg in preparation for on-campus interviews when seeking admission into medical school proved to be invaluable. With our first meeting, which began with him casually taking the time to get to know me, all the while he was formulating a plan for how I could best present myself and my strengths to the interviewers. I was actually pretty surprised when he gave me a "homework assignment," yet it was this preparation between meetings that allowed me to become more comfortable talking about myself, my accomplishments, and the contributions I could make to the incoming class of students. Prior to that first meeting, I was aware of the impressive number of students admitted to the program of their choice after working with Mr. Goldberg. I am pleased to be among his "success stories" and am so very grateful for his commitment to me and so many others through the years in helping each of us realize the first step in the pursuit of our professional goals. His commitment doesn't end there, as he continues to make himself available for progress updates and planning for the next phase of the journey. Mr. Goldberg is truly a generous, selfless man!

—Liam Fischer

———

Mr. Goldberg is a great role model for others. He truly takes time out of his busy schedule so that he can help the youth aspire to reach their ultimate goal of being physicians. Mr. Goldberg has a passion for what he does. He is very personable, approachable, and reliable. He helped me to get into a direct medical program. His advice and preliminary tips are so helpful that it makes you practice and study yourself before the big day. I am so grateful to have Mr. Goldberg as a role model and resource because he truly is a man who is compassionate and helpful toward others.

—Andrew M. Cardoza

———

I had the pleasure of working with Mr. Goldberg while preparing to interview for medical school. Mr. Goldberg coached me in a one-afternoon crash course, teaching me how to highlight my strengths, answer difficult questions, and discuss prior experiences in a meaningful way. He helped refine my interviewing skills so that I would be the best applicant possible and could have meaningful conversations in interviews. He was incredibly accessible and made sure to take time out of his schedule to make sure that I succeeded. I appreciate everything Mr. Goldberg did to help me matriculate into medical school, and I look forward to working with him to strengthen my residency application in the future.

—Alex Glazer

———

Mr. Goldberg is incredibly knowledgeable about medical school admissions and requirements. He is excellent at molding the perfect candidate for medical school. That being said, he does not churn out robots. Rather, he works with students to showcase aspects of our unique personalities and highlights the parts that would make us excellent candidates.

Not only is Mr. Goldberg a source of inspiration with the time and effort he puts into his students, but also inspires us to do much better. I think we've all been reminded that there is always more work to do, but Mr. Goldberg can pinpoint and improve exactly those areas that need more work.

He has helped me from the medical admission essays to the interview, and I can happily say I've been accepted into an incredibly competitive seven-year BS/MD program. I am very grateful for the time he took out of his schedule to help me, and the results truly speak for themselves.

—Katyayini Aribindi

———

The tutoring I received from Mr. Goldberg during the application process was an essential ingredient to my success in gaining admission to the Medical College at Rush University. In fact, when it was time for me to apply for my residency, I once again contacted Mr. Goldberg to consult with him on strategies to gain my ideal residency. I found Mr. Goldberg to be kind, patient, and extremely knowledgeable on the viewpoints of admissions staff. He also has a keen eye for detail which proved to be a fabulous tool for helping me to refine my interview skills and personal statement. If possible, I would suggest that all pre-med students consider utilizing his tutoring services, as well as obtaining a copy of his book for important tips on acing the medical school interview.

—Nathan Pierce

Thank you so much for the help you gave me both revising my personal statement and preparing for an interview! Before working with you, I had applied to medical school twice before and had never even been invited for an interview. This time not only was I invited to the earliest round of interviews, but I was admitted to the University of Illinois at the end of October. Your help and guidance were absolutely invaluable and helped me to succeed. Thank you again!

—Ryder Moses

Mr. Goldberg and the "Goldberg" method were extremely helpful in preparing for medical school interviews. My undergraduate grades weren't amazing, but after talking to Mr. Goldberg, we were able to highlight strengths in my application and use it efficiently during the interview process. I believe that Mr. Goldberg and his interview preparation gave me the confidence to excel during the interview, which in turn, played a crucial role in my acceptance. Thanks again, Mr. Goldberg!

—Michael O'Laughlin

I was referred to Ed Goldberg by my father. Mr. Goldberg had helped my two older sisters with their interviewing skills, and both were admitted to professional schools after benefitting from his aid. Mr. Goldberg had a very "tough love" attitude; he was one hundred percent willing to help me, but he wasn't going to sugar coat anything.

Had it not been for his help, I would not have been so comfortable in my final few interviews, and was accepted to Harvard School of Dental Medicine.

—Matt McShane

As a mature student, I was hesitant about my ability to compete with the large numbers of students applying for medical schools. I was certainly in the minority as an applicant and needed some help from a professional that knows the details about what medical schools are looking for. Luck was on my side when I met Mr. Goldberg, the CEO of St. Alexius Medical Center, in Hoffman Estates, Illinois. He was able to coach me on answers to key questions, my presentation, and my strengths that would tip the scales in my favor. His approach is direct, with unmistakable clarity. Prior to my coaching from Mr. Goldberg, I had applied to numerous medical schools, spending over five thousand dollars on application fees, specific prerequisites, travel to interviews, and professional testing. The result was disappointing and the wait time was aggravating. After consulting with Mr. Goldberg, I applied at my first choice medical school and was notified of my acceptance into their program within ten days. If I had known that he has the ability to know exactly what to do to get into a top notch medical school, I would have hired him two years ago and saved myself a lot of money and grief!

—Diane Roche

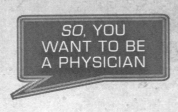

CHAPTER 23
REFERENCE RESOURCES

Exploring a Medical Career

The Association of American Medical Colleges (AAMC) has an article with several questions prospective medical students might ask themselves: Is a medical career right for me? What does it take to be a doctor? What is the career of a physician like? How much do doctors make, how many hours do they work, and what is medical school like? At the time of publication, the article could be found at https://www.aamc.org/students/considering/exploring_medical/.

Get Accepted into Medical School

About.com had an interesting article on this topic on their "Health Careers" page. The article provides helpful tips on how to get into medical school by suggesting that students look beyond just grades and MCAT scores in their efforts to stand out from the crowd. Prospective students can add to their chances of being accepted to medical school by showing their interest in giving back to their community through volunteer roles, leadership positions, and altruism. At the time of publication, the article could be found at http://healthcareers.about.com/od/educationtraining/qt/MDSchoolAccept.htm.

For additional guidance on this subject, the AAMC website provides further information on how to prepare academically for medical school, how to choose the right school for undergraduate education, and how to choose the right medical school. Also discussed are topics such as when a student should apply to medical school, how students should apply, what the MCAT exam is like, and details on what medical schools look for in an applicant and how they decide which individuals to pick. At the time of publication, the article could be found at https://www.aamc.org/students/considering/gettingin/85128/considering_gettingin.html.

The Road to Becoming a Doctor

The AAMC has an extensive brochure on this subject available online. The topics covered include information on the different types of physicians, the medical education process, the length of residency for selected specialties, medical-student debt, and continuing medical education. At the time of publication, the article could be found at https://www.aamc.org/download/68806/data/road-doctor.pdf.

Future Changes to the MCAT

Traci Tillman, a staff reporter for the *Yale Daily News*, summed up the future changes to the MCAT well in her article "Future Pre-Meds Will Take New MCAT." The article discusses the four main MCAT content changes, which include the revamping of the exam's two natural-science sections, the addition of an evaluation of social and behavioral sciences, and the inclusion of ethics and philosophy questions in the verbal-reasoning section. The writing-sample section of the test will be eliminated. At the time of publication, the article could be found at http://www.yaledailynews.com/news/2011/apr/06/future-pre-meds-will-take-new-mcat/.

Preparing for the MCAT

The AAMC provides excellent information on how students should prepare for the MCAT and suggests that students should begin their study plan a minimum of three months before their scheduled exam date. Their website provides details on the exam content, how the exam is scored, and how to select a test date. Students are also told about exam fees, testing rules, and how medical schools use the MCAT scores. At the time of publication, the article could be found at https://www.aamc.org/students/applying/mcat/preparing/85558/study_plan.html.

MCAT Scores and GPAs for Applicants and Matriculants to US Medical Schools

Students who wish to gain a better understanding of what type of grades and scores they need to get into medical school can look at the AAMC's latest research on the topic. The research shows the average MCAT scores by test section and the average GPA of medical-school applicants in comparison to the same data collected on matriculants in 2011. For example, the mean total MCAT score of applicants in 2011 was 28.2, and applicants' mean GPA totals were 3.53. In comparison, the mean total MCAT score of matriculants in 2011 was 31.1, with an average mean GPA total of 3.67. At the time of publication, the research could be found at https://www.aamc.org/download/161692/data/table18.pdf.

For more information about the races and sexes of applicants, acceptees, and matriculants, students can view a variety of tables that outline the results of research conducted by the AAMC. One of the most complete tables, at the time of publication, could be found at https://www.aamc.org/download/161194/data/table12.pdf.

How to Get Off the Medical-School Wait List

Ibrahim Busnaina published an article on October 24, 2011, on www.usnews.com, which provides examples of creative ideas on how students can make the jump from the wait list to becoming a medical-school acceptee. At the time of publication, the article could be found at http://www.usnews.com/education/blogs/medical-school-admissions-doctor/2011/10/24/how-to-get-off-the-medical-school-wait-list.

The Training of Medical Students

Andis Robeznieks, a journalist for *Modern Healthcare*, wrote an interesting article on February 27, 2012, called "New Rounds for Med Students: Revised Admissions Test and a Changing Focus for Essential Skills Will Bring a Fresh Look to Next Generation of Physicians." The article discusses the focus on new cotraining programs with other caregivers and the desire for medical-school students to develop good bedside manners. The article also describes how the public thinks medical schools are doing in educating new doctors and how the new MCAT will affect students. At the time of publication, the article could be found on the *Modern Healthcare* website, www.modernhealthcare.com. Please note that a subscription is needed to view this article.

Medical and Dental Brigades

Participating on brigade to provide medical and dental services for those in need around the world can provide students with invaluable experience, as well as a wider global perspective. There are several groups that facilitate this type of program, but one of the most prominent organizations is Global Brigades. See www.globalbrigades.org/programs.

Identifying Behaviors of Successful Medical-School Students and Residents

The AAMC produced a wonderful publication in 2001 ("Identifying Behaviors of Successful Medical Students and Residents," November 2001, vol. 1, no. 4) that details the attributes that help identify students who would likely become successful physicians. Characteristics examined include skills, values, attitudes, and knowledge.

Residency

A great resource for general information on residency programs can be found on the AAMC website. The PDF publication describes the residency application process and how matching works, and it provides quality suggestions on how to ease the transition from medical school to residency. The information can be found, at the time of publication, at https://members.aamc.org/eweb/upload/Roadmap%20to%20Residency%202ndEd.pdf.

Physician Compensation

There are several articles detailing pay scales for physicians in different specialties, but the best source for information on the topic can be found on the Medical Group Management Association website at http://www.mgma.com/physcomp/.

APPENDIX A

EXAMPLES OF PERSONAL STATEMENTS

Student #1:

First Example from Student #1

The best stories are those that have the most unexpected endings. Fifteen-year-old girls across the world wept when J. K. Rowling killed off their favorite headmaster, and the 2000 US presidential election will go down in history for being decided not by our "error-proof" democracy but by our grandparents and their sun-kissed neighbors in Florida. The surprising plot twists of both *New York Times* best sellers and real everyday lives are what make us jump out of our seats and do a Jersey Shore fist pump before all rationality can tell us to hold back. While I may not know what ending the fortune-cookie gods have in store for me, I do know that I plan on making my life anything but ordinary.

I did a good job standing out right off the bat, or better yet, right out of the womb. Though having been beaten in subsequent years, I was once one of the youngest patients at Children's Memorial Hospital in Chicago to undergo dermatologic laser surgery. Being poked and prodded by medical professionals at such an early age, it's no wonder that the last thing I wanted was to become a doctor. No, I wanted to be a singer…then a dancer…then an Olympic swimmer. Scratch that, Olympic diver. After all, they got to spin in the air. But thanks to Newton and those silly laws of physics, being an international diving sensation just was not in the cards for me. I became a wandering nomad in the abyss of undetermined majors and uncertain futures called adolescence.

Then in the summer of 2009, I had the opportunity to travel to Israel with my two best friends through a program called Birthright. The trip is aimed to help young Jewish people learn about their religious and cultural identity through experience rather than narration. Like my first kiss, Israel opened my eyes to a whole new side of life. Exhilarating and welcoming, one could only laugh at the thought that one had never experienced such pure, chaotic happiness before. I was no longer on the outside of a closed door, wishing to understand that wet, uncoordinated initiation of love. I was finally inside the room smiling from ear to ear. I loved everything, from the pushy pedestrians at the bus stop unafraid to step on your toes to get on first to the sleek oil in the Israeli cuisine, whether in the familiar hummus and pita or the "I don't recognize this meat" special that slipped out just as easily as it slipped in. For the first time, I loved something for myself, something out of my own conviction, rather than through my inheritance. Don't get me wrong, I love my family, but all my interests, all the major loves of my life—sports, science,

Adam Sandler movies—all of them were characteristics of my last name, rather than my first. For me, Israel was my first taste of originality, of having my own extraordinary plan. I promised myself from then on that I would pursue what made me happy, no matter the inevitable vulnerability and fear that accompanies stepping out on your own.

My junior year I went back to Israel hand in hand with vulnerability and fear as a part of a study-abroad class through the University of Illinois with eighteen other students I didn't know. Eighteen other students who weren't Jewish, eighteen other students who had no idea what Birthright was. Therefore, when everyone was as excited as I was when we boarded the bus after our visit to Gesher Al Wadi Elementary School, I knew the pride I felt wasn't just a Jewish thing, but rather a human thing. Gesher Al Wadi is one of only four very unique schools in the state of Israel. What's so special about these schools? Well, these schools are bilingual schools. That's right—Arabic and Hebrew are spoken, and taught, in the very same classroom, beginning in kindergarten. Children from both sides of the conflict get the opportunity to learn about each other in a positive environment instead of the kind of situations you see on the news or hear on TV. When the third-grade class beat the fourth-grade class in a competitive soccer match, there was quite the celebration. Dr. A., the vice principal of the school, laughed as he told us, "When you ask the winners how they did it, the Jewish kids answered because their Arab friends were so good and the Arab kids answered because their Jewish friends were so good." As Dr. A. showed me, all it takes to change the world is one new idea. All it took to change my world was one new option.

My father and uncle are successful pediatricians in the suburbs of Chicago. I got the wonderful pleasure of inheriting a summer job in my father's office. My job title was medical assistant. As a medical assistant, you are right there in the action. You put the patient in the room, take vitals, record any problems, perform tests, and give vaccines. Premed friends of mine would kill for this kind of experience. For two years I was indifferent to working there. The repetition of the job was agonizing to me. Soon after starting, a robot version of me was born, merely floating through the everyday motions. Charting and giving routine shots was not interesting, and listening to crying babies definitely was not fun.

Then last summer, my uncle brought me in a room during an examination. I thought he just wanted me to help hold the child so he could continue his examination, but instead he asked me, "What do you see on the patient?"

I counted all the fingers and all the toes, checked the number of limbs, and then proceeded to stare at my uncle in all seriousness and say, "A baby."

He laughed and said, "Look harder."

So I looked at the baby's face—two eyes, nose, and mouth—check. I just smiled and said, "A very handsome baby." Now the mom was smiling. My uncle pointed to the patient's neck. On the left side, there was a massive lump. My uncle referred to it as a benign cyst. All I could muster was a half-hearted, "Cool," while figuratively hitting myself on the head. How could I have missed such an obvious deviation from normal?

When we left the room, my uncle said, "The most important thing any good doctor can do in an examination is look at the patient. By just looking you get more information than any test can give you." After that, medicine got interesting.

In the same summer, I had the pleasure of meeting one of my dad's favorite patients, Elliott. Elliott is an adolescent boy with Down syndrome. Elliott was put in a room like every other patient, but when my dad went in the room, something out of the ordinary happened. Over the intercom, my dad said, "Paging Dr. Elliott, paging Dr. Elliott, you are needed in room two." Since we don't have a Dr. Elliott and it wasn't too busy, I joined my dad in the patient's room to see what all the noise was about. After all, I would have rather done anything than file more lab results. I watched as my dad took his stethoscope off of his neck and put it correctly on Elliott. If Elliott was going to be a doctor, he needed the proper equipment. When Elliott heard the lubb-dupp of my dad's heart, the only smile bigger than Elliott's was that of his mom. My dad showed me for the first time that medicine can be fun. The relationships with the patients, the ability to help the five-year-old girl with the tiara believe she is a princess for one more day, or the hug you give the modest high-school grad that has come a long way from kicking the door at the sight of needles—that is where the fun is.

From my family I have learned the virtues and ideals that I hold dear, but it is from my own conviction that I have decided to pursue a career in medicine. In no other field can I find a perfect blend of exact science and creativity that so greatly matches my interests. From a few life experiences, I have found that pushing my own personal boundaries and taking a few independent steps, no matter how lonely they may seem, have proven to be the most rewarding and effective. Although I do not know where my story will end, I know that my insistence on bettering myself and my life will make one great story, full of the unexpected.

Comments:
* Another student I believe trying to be cute. I loved all of the J. K. Rowling movies, but the reference to Harry Potter *is not cute, at least not to me. Some* Harry Potter*–loving professionals might like it, but I think the risk is too high.*
* The comment about the election and "sun-kissed" neighbors in Florida is terrible. I recommend never talking about politics.

* The Jersey Shore fist pump! What academic physician on
an admissions committee would not be offended?
* Why would anyone say they wanted to be anything other than a physician? A singer,
a dancer, an Olympic diver—none of them are even science- or service-related.
* Talking about religion is as bad as talking about poli-
tics unless it's a mission trip helping people. Please don't.
* The medical experience was great and was worked into the final draft.

Second Example from Student #1

"Our job is improving the quality of life, not just delaying death. Why can't we treat death with a certain amount of humanity and dignity, and decency, and God forbid, maybe even humor? Death is not the enemy, gentlemen. If we're going to fight a disease, let's fight one of the most terrible diseases of all, indifference."

—*Patch Adams*

Working in my dad and uncle's pediatric office in the suburbs of Chicago over the last four summers, I have had the privilege of seeing many aspects of the medical world that other premed students would probably give an arm and a leg for. As a medical assistant, I do anything and everything to help my dad and uncle get through the day efficiently and effectively, whether that means running a strep test or giving well-visit vaccines. Despite all my responsibilities, my favorite job, as my uncle likes to remind me, is "owwee" control coordinator and lollipop distributor. He says I am the reason why the lollipop industry will never be going into recession. I smile and say, "Good thing you don't give away iPods."

My lollipop enthusiasm probably comes from my upbringing. At a very young age, I was shown the immeasurable distance a little good deed could travel. From first grade to high school, I belonged to the Kindness Club, a group of girls dedicated to helping various causes on a monthly basis. Over the years we did everything from raising money to train a Seeing Eye dog to sewing over twenty blankets to donate to Project Linus, a nonprofit organization whose mission is to "provide love, a sense of security, warmth, and comfort to children who are seriously ill, traumatized, or otherwise in need." If you asked me as a twelve-year-old what it felt like to do these activities, I would tell you it felt good. However, not until I was older did I discover how much helping others would help me.

In the fall of 2008, I was a bright-eyed college freshman ready to embrace the best four years of my life. I would make lots of friends, do well in school, and mature into a sophisticated individual in an environment away from home. Unfortunately, I was not prepared for the stress of living a life totally dedicated to the needs of one person—myself. For the first time in my life, I was completely and totally responsible for my actions and well-being. I didn't have to coordinate dinner plans with my parents. Even scarier, I was now in charge of my own laundry, bleach and softener included. I was completely immersed in my own life and my life alone. It was in this selfish lifestyle that I became uninterested in my life and, in effect, totally miserable. I would sleep all day to avoid the indifference I felt, the kind of indifference that makes one think, "What's the point?" Once my dad caught wind of what was going on, he made me come home to see a specialist. In March 2009 during my second semester in college, I was diagnosed with an adjustment disorder heading toward depression. That day I decided it was time for me to change the way I was living. I needed to free myself of my vanity and take the focus off of myself. W. B. Yeats once wrote, "Only God, my dear, could love you for yourself alone and not your yellow hair." The same day I visited my psychologist, I walked into a local hair salon and cut off ten inches of my hair to be donated to Locks of Love. An immeasurable weight was lifted off of my shoulders, literally, and on that day I started to feel better.

Growing up as the daughter of a pediatrician and the sister of a medical-school student, I was originally hesitant to put all my eggs in the "future doctor" basket because I did not want to go into the field for the wrong reason—familiarity. I wanted to pave my own way, and as such I have dabbled in some other fields of expertise, like book editing and global relations. However, despite my best efforts, something has always brought me back to medicine. In no other field can I find a perfect blend of exact science and compassion toward others that so greatly matches my passion.

In high school I had the chance to pick my own classes for the first time. Science and math always had a pull on me, but the upper-level sciences, as I would reassert in college, carried a whole new level of intrigue. High school also taught me the art of prioritizing and multitasking. Being a three-year varsity athlete, it wasn't always easy finding time for school, family, and friends. Despite some trying times, I was able to perform well both on the field, receiving All-Conference and All-Area recognition, as well as in the classroom, graduating with a weighted GPA of 4.52 and winning the Athletic Academic Award, given to three senior athletes with the top three GPAs.

In college I continued to explore my passion of science, specifically chemistry. In the fall of my junior year, I joined a very successful research group under the guidance and supervision of Dr. S. With the help of the team and my wonderful graduate-student supervisor, Mr. O., I have learned a great deal about inorganic chemistry, its applications (medical and otherwise), and its infinite potential to help the world. I am writing a senior thesis about my two years of research in the group.

I found that, at school, my freedom and independence allowed me more time for some of my hobbies. Freshman year I was elected the president of Shi-Ai, a philanthropic organization that consists of members from all sororities on campus. Single-handedly, I created a fund-raiser for the Champaign Humane Society called "Pennies for Puppies" that was so successful it became an annual event for the organization. Sophomore year I started work on implementing the body-image program into my sorority. The body-image program is the first scientifically supported, evidence-based eating disorders prevention program designed for and with sororities. The program, Reflections, endeavors to help participants resist the unrealistic ideal ultrathin standard of female beauty prevalent in today's society. Self-esteem is such a huge issue for young women and a struggle very close to my heart. So when my friend in a different sorority told me about the body-image program, I had to get involved. After two years of meetings, paperwork, and training, the program was finally implemented in the fall of 2009. Sophomore year was also the year I decided to try out for the women's club softball team at U of I. Freshman year I had decided to hang up my cleats after twelve years with the idea that it was time to move on. Unfortunately, my heart and my bat were not ready to give up, and what followed was the best season of my life.

Comment:
* *Maybe only 5 percent of all physicians would appreciate the Patch Adams reference, approximately 70 percent would disapprove, and 25 percent might not care. Why risk it?*
* *Keep your personal laundry at home—don't volunteer it.*

Third Example from Student #1

I have known three things since an early age. I feel better about myself when I help others, particularly children; I enjoy science, particularly chemistry; and being a physician would allow me to actively help people in an area that is so important, their health.

From first grade through high school, I belonged to the Kindness Club, a group of girls dedicated to helping various causes on a monthly basis. Over the years we did everything from raising money and training a Seeing Eye dog to sewing more than twenty blankets to donate to Project Linus, a nonprofit organization whose mission is to provide love, a sense of security, and comfort to children who are seriously ill, traumatized, or otherwise in need.

I graduated high school with a weighted grade point average of 4.52 out of 4.00. I played three years of varsity softball and was the MVP of the softball team and awarded the achievement award for the athlete with the highest GPA at my school. At a very young age, I was shown the immeasurable distance that a good deed could travel.

At the U of I, I was the president of Shi-Ai, which is a group that performs philanthropic activities through Champaign-Urbana and is made up of all members of the twenty sororities on campus. I created "Pennies for Puppies," a fund-raiser for the local dog shelter. Because of the success of the event, it became an annual event.

I believe that many women, including me, have struggled with their weight and all that goes along with being a "bigger girl," and I became the body-image coordinator from my sorority and spent two years implementing the program.

I continued my interest in science at the University of Illinois as a chemistry major with a minor in English and achieved a 3.7 grade point average out of a possible 4.0.

I have shadowed Dr. C., a pediatric ophthalmologist, as well as Dr. M., a pediatric infectious-disease physician, which was very exciting, educational, and consistent with my goal of helping children.

I have performed and am currently in the process of performing research for Professor S., an extremely successful inorganic-chemistry researcher and one of the reasons the University of Illinois chemistry graduate program is in the top five of the nation. I am under the supervision of Mr. O., a graduate student, and together we are trying to create superparamagnetic nanoparticles for drug delivery using Professor S.'s ultrasonic spray paralysis. I am writing a senior thesis based on my two years of research in Dr. S.'s lab. Despite the broken glass, it's extremely rewarding because the research is aimed at bettering the world and helping others through technology.

I believe a significant factor that has encouraged me to be a physician is working with my father and uncle as a medical assistant in their office. They are successful pediatricians in the suburbs of Chicago. As a medical assistant, you are right there in the action. You put the patient in the room, take vitals, record any problems, perform tests, and give vaccines. I can safely hold a kicking and screaming child in my sleep.

Last summer, my uncle brought me in a room during an examination. I thought he just wanted me to help hold the child so he could continue his examination. Instead he asked me, "What do you see on the patient?"

I counted all the fingers and all the toes, checked the number of limbs, and proceeded to stare at my uncle with all seriousness and say, "A baby."

He laughed and said, "Look harder," so I looked at the baby's face: two eyes, a nose, and mouth—check.

I just smiled and said, "A very handsome baby," and now the mom was smiling. My uncle pointed to the patient's neck. On the left side there was a massive lump, and my uncle referred to it as a benign cyst. All I could muster was a half-hearted, "Ohhhh," while figuratively hitting myself on the head. How could I have missed such an obvious deviation from normal?

When we left the room, Uncle Sam told me, "One of the most important functions any good doctor can perform in an examination is to look at the patient; just by looking you get more information than many tests can provide." After that, my interest in medicine was heightened.

I also had the pleasure of meeting one of my dad's favorite patients, Elliott, who is an adolescent boy with Down syndrome. Elliott was put in a room like every other patient, but when Dad went into the room, something out of the ordinary happened. Over the intercom, my dad said, "Paging Doctor Elliott—paging Doctor Elliott—you are needed in room two." Since we don't have a Doctor Elliott and it wasn't too busy, I joined my dad in the patient's room to see what all the noise was about. I watched as my dad took his stethoscope off his neck and put it directly on Elliott. If Elliott was going to be a doctor, he needed the proper equipment. When Elliott heard the lubb-dupp of my dad's heart, the only smile bigger than Elliott's was that of his mother. My dad showed medicine could be fun for the patient and help to engage him in working together in ensuring or improving his health. The relationships with the patients, the ability to help the five-year-old girl with a tiara believe she is a princess for one more day, and receiving a hug from the modest high-school grad that has come a long way from kicking the door at the sight of needles is where the personal reward comes from. This is what motivates and excites me.

I recognize that medicine is a profession that requires vigorous attainment of knowledge and expertise. From my family, I have learned the virtues and ideals that I hold dear, but it is through my own conviction that I decided to pursue a career in medicine. In no other field can I find a perfect blend of exact science and compassion toward others that so greatly matches my passion.

One of my favorite jobs, as my uncle likes to remind me, is "owwee" control coordinator and lollipop distributor. I believe my lollipop enthusiasm combined with a caring, empathic attitude demonstrates full circle the immeasurable distance a good deed can travel.

I believe medicine is the greatest medium in which people can help others. Whether it is showing a child with Down syndrome how to use a stethoscope so he wouldn't be afraid of it, or boosting the confidence of a ten-year-old girl when her eye doctor tells her how beautiful she looks in her new glasses. I want to be a physician, not only because I want to help people but because I want to engage with people and be touched by their lives as I can hopefully touch theirs. I want to be a physician who treats the human condition, not just the illness. I want to bring warmth, compassion, and perhaps laughter to help gain the patient's trust. If I have the honor of receiving an invitation to your medical school, I know I will carry with me the lessons of pursuing greatness through compassion, warmth, and hard work. After all, sometimes all it takes is a lollipop, a little magic, and warmth.

Comment: Same student, different draft. I loved the office experience and importance of humanness. I would have left off some of the personal and extracurricular activities not relevant to medical school.

Fourth Example from Student #1

From first grade through high school, I belonged to the Kindness Club, a girls' volunteer group dedicated to helping various causes on a monthly basis. We did everything from raising money to train a Seeing Eye dog to sewing blankets for donations aimed at helping seriously ill or traumatized children. My involvement in the Kindness Club deeply ingrained a passion for giving within me, and it was not until I formalized my decision to become a doctor that I realized the true value of these experiences in my youth.

Upon reaching high school, I was thrilled to finally choose my courses. Science and math had always piqued my interest, so I challenged myself in Advanced Placement sciences, which heightened my level of intrigue. While the coursework kept me busy, I was not hesitant to explore other talents and interests. Varsity athletics filled my schedule for three years, and I was forced to develop a way to prioritize and allow time to develop socially. Admittedly, difficulties arose, but I routinely found solace in the notion that my hard work would one day allow me to pursue my passion of giving. With this strengthened determination, I performed well in athletics, receiving All-Conference and All-Area recognition, as well as in the classroom, graduating with a weighted GPA of 4.52 and winning the Athletic Academic Award, which was given to only three senior athletes with the top GPAs.

Entering college, I continued exploring science, specifically chemistry. In my junior year, I joined Dr. S. in his student research group. Along with the research team, I have had the unique opportunity to apply my knowledge of inorganic chemistry in a real research environment. Because of this experience, I have become fascinated with its applications (medical and otherwise), as well as its great potential to better our world.

Over the past three summers, I have worked in my father and uncle's pediatric office in the suburbs of Chicago. As a medical assistant, I contribute wherever Dad or Uncle Sam need me to, from performing strep tests to administering well-visit vaccines. While developing an understanding of the logistics had been interesting, it is without a doubt my response to witnessing patient interactions that proves medicine is the right path for me.

One of my dad's patients, an adolescent boy, Elliott, with Down syndrome, made a memorable visit my first summer. The boy was assigned to a room like every other patient, but when Dad entered the room, something out of the ordinary happened. Over the intercom I heard my father's voice: "Paging Doctor Elliott—paging Doctor Elliott—you are needed in room two." Out of pure curiosity, I joined my dad in the patient's room. My eyes were fixated as he placed his stethoscope around Elliott's neck. Surely, if Elliott was going to be the doctor, he needed the proper equipment. When Elliott heard the lubb-dupp of my dad's heart, I quickly noticed that the only smile in that room bigger than Elliott's was that of his mother.

In that moment my dad showed me that medicine could bring joy to the patient, something I rarely realized as a serious science student. More importantly, I saw that, as a doctor, engaging patients is not simply for fun—it is crucial. Building strong patient-doctor relationships, convincing the five-year-old girl with a tiara that she is a princess, or hugging the mature high-school graduate that once sat kicking the door in fear of needles brings an indescribable reward. These memories are my motivation.

I recognize that medicine is a profession that requires vigorous attainment of knowledge and expertise. From my family I have learned the necessity of this profession, but it is through my own conviction that I have decided to pursue a career in medicine. Medicine, I believe, is the greatest medium in which kindness is achieved. My childhood experiences in the Kindness Club leap to the surface of my mind because the intense feelings of gratification, pride, and confidence involved in giving have driven me to this point.

I want to be a doctor not only because I am confident in my knowledge of science but because I want to engage people and be touched by their lives—as I can hopefully touch theirs. I want to be a physician who treats the human condition, not just the illness. Along with precision I will bring warmth, compassion, and perhaps laughter to the everyday patient-doctor interactions.

I thank you for considering my application, and if I have the honor of receiving an invitation to your medical school, I will carry with me the lesson of pursuing greatness through passion, dedication, and hard work.

Comment: Good discussion of the human experience of working with patients. Accepted into the medical school of her choice. This woman had the grades, MCAT score, service, and poise to get in. Why risk it all with an out-there, too-creative, too-funny personal statement?

—

Student #2

I decided to become a physician later than most. This was not due to a lack of exposure; my mother is a pediatric anesthesiologist. I was born while she was in medical school and my sister while she was in residency. With my dad working around the country, we were raised during those early years mostly by her parents. Nevertheless, I still admire my mom more than any woman I know. She works harder than I can possibly imagine, and her stories of interesting patients, close saves, and terrible losses were inspiring. But her long hours and time spent away from home always rankled, as did her bitter, openly stated regret at not being there as her children grew up. Thus, in high school, I focused more on math and physics and tried to avoid biology as much as possible. Once I got to college, I thought my career was set. I liked machines, outer space, and things that go boom—rocket science it was.

I also felt that I owed something back to the society that had given me so much while I was growing up, compared to what I saw during family trips to India. The grinding poverty was evident while driving along dusty roads to visit my father's birth town: cripples on every street corner and rail-thin children and families living under threat from zealots of all stripes. I decided to join Air Force ROTC and pay back some of the debt that I owed to my country for giving me a childhood free from danger and hunger.

Life had different plans. I joined MIT's student-run ambulance service on a lark; driving with lights and sirens screaming through Boston seemed like a fun thing to do. And indeed it was, but not for the reason I was expecting. By day, I would sit in class, taking notes, solving equations. But nights and weekends, my job went from adding and subtracting numbers to taking care of people. To the considerable relief of my supervisors, I rapidly lost the desire to hit sixty miles per hour going against traffic on a one-way street, responding to a patient with an isolated ankle injury. But I am still deeply honored that patients of all ages, races, and sexes would respect and trust me, then a nineteen-year-old college student, to take care of them.

The summer after freshman year, due to AFROTC's training requirements, I looked for a flexible job that would allow me to leave in the middle to go to an air base in Alaska. My own PCP had an opening and gave me a shot. She had recently made the transition to EMR and needed someone to enter patient data. As I was an EMT, she also had me take vitals, HPIs, AMPLE history, and notes in the room while she talked to the patient, and assist her in her minor office procedures. Needless to say, holding the basin while she performed ear irrigations and testing urine samples wasn't the most glamorous stuff. But the patients' smiles and heartfelt thank-yous after we had treated them as best we could were more uplifting than I could have imagined. Lengthening and improving other people's lives was my job—it was one of the most rewarding things I had ever done.

Two events finally made me settle on medicine. First, I completed an internship at MIT Lincoln Laboratories doing aerospace software design for national defense. My colleagues were smart and great to work with, and the work was challenging and interesting. But while my work engaged my intellectual capacities, it didn't feel that meaningful. Aerospace engineering as a whole up to this point had been fun. I still remember the fierce rush of pride as the RC plane my team designed and built flew for the first time (though it was soon mitigated by horror as the six-foot foam wing broke in half upon landing, necessitating frantic resuscitation attempts as the plane was due for a grade in forty-eight hours). But while engineering was fun, it was never as fulfilling as my medical experiences.

Soon after, I found out that my mother had been diagnosed with lupus. I understood little about the disease, but I did know the prognosis included flares and organ failure. With hospital stays on the horizon, I couldn't commission into the air force and be unable to visit her should she suffer from flares in the future; the nearest air-force base is five hundred miles away from home. I made the painful decision to withdraw from AFROTC. Furthermore, her illness made me realize even more how much relief and joy doctors bring not only to their patients but to their patients' loved ones as well. I made the decision to start the long road to becoming a physician.

Switching courses has been neither fun nor easy, as I find myself competing with freshmen and sophomores and taking summer courses to complete both my aerospace degree and premedical requirements on time. I understand all too well the personal sacrifices that I am making and that I am forcing my future family to make. But I've realized that my engineering background is still useful in designing and evaluating both medical devices and organizations, as well as developing technology to better deliver care. And more than anything, I am looking forward to the day I will have patients of my own. While I am apprehensive of the great responsibility, I know the payoff, their smiling faces, is well worth the cost.

Comment: I suggested several changes, only a few of which were accepted by the student. I didn't like the reference to the ambulance service as a "lark" and "seem[ing]" like a fun thing to do." I also felt having many career changes was not beneficial. All that being said, a thirty-eight on the MCAT spoke for itself.

Student #3

In its mission statement, the UIC Honors College is described as a community of scholars whose goal is to enrich the educational experience of undergraduates and allow faculty and students of all disciplines to interact in teaching, learning, and research. What scholarly attributes do you bring to this community, and what do you expect in return?

As I sat listening to the University of Illinois Chicago's Honors College presentation one chilly November morning, I envisioned myself as a student on campus. I was impressed by the abundance and variance of research opportunities and found myself avidly taking notes about the prospects of engaging in honors coursework and participating in student organizations that I knew would help enrich my college education. I feel that my scholarly credentials qualify me for consideration into the UIC honors track. Not only do I have the academic tenacity needed to take on such a stimulating curriculum, but also the experiences I have been able to garner for my past seventeen years of existence have allowed me to become an open-minded, creative, and compassionate leader, ready to tackle the challenges of the academic world.

My strongest and perhaps most utilized trait is my sense of open-mindedness. Because my mother is an employee of United Airlines, I have been fortunate enough to journey to six of the seven world continents. My many sojourns have allowed me to witness how others across the globe spend their days and have also given me the opportunity to respect the various cultural and social differences that set us apart. One instance that particularly stands out in my mind is my first exposure to poverty, which occurred while I was in India. Actually walking among these individuals and witnessing their stark living conditions increased my awareness of social disparity on both a local and global level. I carry this awareness into my personal life at home as I try to empathize with my fellow classmates and teachers. This trait especially helps me with the leadership roles that I hold, both in my school and community, as it gives me greater ability to understand others' wants and needs. This trait will hopefully carry over at UIC and allow me to accept cultural and social differences that I may encounter in the university's highly diverse student body. I also envision that this trait will help me in my future career. As a potential doctor, my open-mindedness will allow me to relate and empathize with my patients.

The long hours I put into my school newspaper as presiding editor in chief, coupled with the speeches I regularly deliver as speech captain, exemplify my sense of creativity. In both activities I had to learn not only how to effectively motivate a group to perform at their best but also the importance of thinking "out of the box" and reasoning with others' viewpoints in comparison to my own. To me, the prospect of being able to present information in a manner that I feel will captivate the minds of a twenty-five-hundred-member student body excites me and pushes me to find innovative means to do so. At UIC, I plan to take advantage of this passion by writing for one of the student-organized honor journals, such as *JPHAS* or *Ampersand*. I want to be able to touch the minds of my fellow students, as well as the surrounding community, in a useful manner and feel that these outlets would help me do so.

I will bring this sense of creativity to UIC through my literary activities and also through my experience as a choreographer for the Indian Dance Academy, which I have been a part of for the past nine years. Dancing is my most valued extracurricular activity, and I am extremely thankful for having been given the opportunity to explore my roots, as well as the cultural practices of my Hindu ancestors. Through my experiences with dance, I participated in a variety of cultural showcases and talent competitions and was even given the opportunity to dance at the India's Independence Day Parade in Chicago for the past two years, as well as in the Museum of Science and Industry's Holidays around the World Showcase. More importantly, however, I danced for various social causes, such as cancer awareness and global poverty benefits. Through these events I garnered a sense of compassion for worldly affairs and learned how to incorporate my hobbies in order to make a greater impact on my community as a whole. At UIC, I hope to use my talents toward a similar cause, perhaps organizing a cultural charity event that would benefit both the campus community and a larger part of society.

The only thing I ask in return from the UIC campus and faculty is to provide me with a stimulating environment that will allow me to continue developing my talents and explore different aspects of my academic and professional interests. As an aspiring doctor, I feel that the GPPA program will allow me to gain unmatched experience within the medical field. The vast patient demographics and medical situations that await me at the Illinois Medical District cannot be found with any other institution, which is why I will gain more quality experience as a student here. I am confident that UIC will allow me to reach my professional ambition in a successful manner.

Comment: I suggested to the student that there was not enough science and too much newspaper and dance. Outside interests are fine, but they should not detract from the core of science classes. The student rejected my suggestions.

First Example from Student #4

I have always been fascinated by everything scientific, especially the function and complexity of living things. A strong sense of curiosity defined by a desire to understand constantly encourages me to learn more and is one reason I want to pursue a career in medicine. I have always been interested in the intricacies of systems and pathways within the human physiology, and the prospect of being able to interact with and repair these systems greatly excites me. The challenge of being able to directly affect and work to heal the human body is one that I dream of mastering; however, the opportunity to build personal connections by helping people is the primary reason I am interested in medicine.

In addition to a love of learning and excitement about medicine, my personality and general demeanor will also help me to be a compassionate physician. First, I excel when challenged and have strong problem-solving skills. My experiences while living in Japan were a true test of my abilities. When I first arrived, I had only a basic knowledge of the language. Even though I continued my studies, the challenges of integrating into such a different culture truly tested me. The Japanese language has thousands of kanji characters, making common tasks like grocery shopping difficult. Every day was a new adventure, and I thrived knowing that everything around me would yield new challenges that needed to be understood and solved. My time in Japan also helped me to understand how focused I am and how I always strive to exceed expectations through hard work and perseverance. By the end of my stay, I was able to interact with Japanese people and form lasting friendships.

After returning, I carried these invaluable experiences with me as I continued my academic pursuits. Ever enthusiastic about science and the acquisition of knowledge, my fascination was constantly stoked by the experiences I had working with a cardiologist. By observing and learning tests and techniques commonly used to diagnose ailments, as well as how these medical problems are addressed, my desire to become a doctor was heightened. I understand and appreciate the level of skill and dedication required to become a physician. I believe my enthusiasm, determination, general caring, and accessible nature will help me to learn and embody these ideals.

Comment: I suggested mentioning more facts, GPA, and the MCAT. There was no research or experience to draw from.

Second Example from Student #4

I have always been fascinated by everything scientific, especially the function and complexity of living things. A strong sense of curiosity, defined by a desire to understand, constantly encourages me to learn more and is one reason I want to pursue a career in medicine. I have always been interested in the intricacies of systems and pathways within the human physiology, and the prospect of being able to interact with and repair these systems greatly excites me. The challenge of being able to directly affect and work to heal the human body is one that I dream of mastering; however, the opportunity to build personal connections by helping people is the primary reason I am interested in medicine.

In addition to a love of learning and excitement about medicine, my personality and general demeanor will also help me to be a compassionate physician. First, I excel when challenged and have strong problem-solving skills. My experiences while living in Japan were a true test of my abilities. When I first arrived, I had only a basic knowledge of the language. Even though I continued my studies, the challenges of integrating into such a different culture truly tested me. The Japanese language has thousands of kanji characters, making common tasks like grocery shopping difficult. Every day was a new adventure, and I thrived knowing that everything around me would yield new challenges that needed to be understood and solved. My time in Japan also helped me to understand how focused I am and how I always strive to exceed expectations through hard work and perseverance. By the end of my stay, I was able to interact with Japanese people and form lasting friendships.

After returning, I carried these invaluable experiences with me as I continued my academic pursuits. Ever enthusiastic about science and the acquisition of knowledge, my fascination was constantly stoked by the experiences I had working with a cardiologist. Since graduating from college, I have been pursuing a master's degree in biotechnology and chemical sciences. During the 2011 spring semester, I participated in a medical internship that involved shadowing doctors in a variety of specialties every week.

By observing and learning tests and techniques commonly used to diagnose ailments, as well as how these medical problems are addressed, my desire to become a doctor was heightened. I understand and appreciate the level of skill and dedication required to become a physician. I believe my enthusiasm, determination, general caring, and accessible nature will help me to learn and embody these ideals.

Comment: Better, but still lacking additional info, GPA, and the MCAT.

First Example from Student #5

I aspired to be a physician after coming to the realization that not everyone can be the Pink Time Force (Power) Ranger. By the time I graduated from college, I had extensive knowledge of gas chromatography / mass spectrometry and how to conduct organic synthesis via microwave radiation. During my years in college, I had gained a strong passion for biomedical research; participating in research was relaxing for me. I liked it immediately. My first day in the lab, I decided that research was going to be one of my preferred extracurricular activities while in college. Engaging in research strengthened my cognitive and leadership skills, while enhancing my confidence in performing presentations. In addition to my coursework and research, I was the president of Chemistry Society for two years, during which time the organization participated in numerous academic and social activities. I also had the opportunity to travel and present my research at symposiums and national meetings organized by the American Chemical Society, allowing me the opportunity to meet renowned chemists from across the nation. While my window for having a future in research was wide open, I continued to be a determined aspiring physician.

With a solid academic background after graduation I decided to focus on expanding my healthcare experience. I was employed by PhysAssist Scribes Inc., and in my first few months I saw multiple traumas from motor-vehicle collisions, myocardial infarctions, appendicitis, and small bowel obstructions, as well as many other emergency cases, and observed physicians making clinical decisions. Furthermore, I learned how to properly document medical records and became experienced using various electronic medical record systems. The greatest joy was when I was promoted to be a certified trainer scribe followed by the position of a lead trainer and started traveling to cities around the nation to train.

By the time I was a lead trainer, I had become an expert in my workforce. I had increased my medical understanding, the communicator between physician and patient, and developed a strong sense of leadership and improved my communication skills. I engage with physicians on a daily basis and have started many scribe programs in various cities in the Midwest. Starting a program involves working with corporate physician groups and the hospitals on successfully carrying out contracts, while initiating and stabilizing a productive program. The programs I have worked on have expanded after implementation, allowing me to have multiple facilities under my wing at any given time. My work has become such an integral part of my life that, similar to research, going to the hospital and doing clinical shifts and holding classroom trainings for the new scribes has been very fulfilling. This is primarily because my employment has allowed me the opportunity to travel, work with emergency physicians in different facilities, and gain insight into the practice of medicine while ensuring me of my career interest in the field of medicine.

My time spent traveling has allowed me to think about what inspires me to be a physician. I learned that research demands determination, dedication, courage, and strength, which are some of the defining characteristics of an ideal physician. Research interested and challenged me. By working on drug-synthesis projects, I understood more about how research scientists are able to make important breakthroughs. The research and clinical aspects of medicine work in unison, while ensuring that both combined are carried out in the best interest of the patient. My experience as a scribe in the health-care field has strengthened my initial intent to be a physician because in physicians I see the empathy and compassion I desire in my career. During each shift I think to myself…this is the reason I want to be a doctor. I want to engage with patients and solve problems to help them through their crises. I want to be in an environment where I will be challenged constantly for the benefit of others.

Comment: Reference to Power Rangers not a good idea. I think the student thought he was trying to be cute. Not cute—to me at least.

Second Example from Student #5

As a high-school senior, I was accepted into the Health Professions Recruitment and Exposure Program at the University of Texas–Southwestern Medical School, which exposed young students to the possibility of a career in health care. From anatomy to microbiology, we learned to explore the human body through the lens of science. The more I learned, the more I became fascinated. Every day was a new adventure in this program. We experienced a simulated childbirth, substituting red Kool-Aid for blood; we watched videos on how the circulatory system worked; and we read about how cells engineered energy from oxygen and glucose (brilliant!). In my final days of high school, I was certain I had to explore science and medicine during my college years.

In college, I took part in a myriad of activities, from the Indian-Pakistani Student Association to election as a residential senator in student government, all of which helped me begin developing leadership skills I would appreciate years down the line. I was accepted into the biomedical research support program, where I worked under an organic chemist, assisting in the synthesis of bisamidoximes, a chemical being explored as an anticancer agent. As I learned how to conduct scientific research, write grant proposals, and share findings with my peers, I began to appreciate the role of research in medicine. Soon, biomedical research began evolving into an important element of my future career.

Engaging in research challenged me to ask the right questions and develop a plan to get answers. It strengthened my cognitive skills and helped me build confidence in presenting information to colleagues. With my early successes in bench research, I was offered an opportunity to complete an accelerated master's degree in chemistry at Southern Methodist University. During this time, I kept a strong commitment to community service beyond the bench, serving as president of the Chemistry Society for two years. As president, I took initiative to mentor our members and find opportunities to improve the campus environment through talks and educational activities about chemistry (our work culminated in our organization being formally recognized by the American Chemical Society). I also had the opportunity to travel and present my research at symposiums and national meetings organized by the American Chemical Society, allowing me the chance to meet and learn from renowned chemists from across the nation. By the time I graduated, I was proficient with gas chromatography / mass spectrometry and knew how to conduct organic-synthesis experiments via microwave radiation. I began to see that it took more than bench acumen to be a great researcher; it also took leadership, courage, empathy, curiosity, strength, and determination.

However, I still thirsted for a more direct, person-to-person service component to my career that research alone could not offer. I turned my focus to health care and applied for a position as a medical scribe in the emergency room with PhysAssist Scribes Inc. My job was to work alongside emergency physicians to help them document patient medical charts. This experience gave me a fascinating and intimate window into patient care, which motivated me to be the best scribe I could be. Soon I was promoted to be a certified trainer scribe and then to the position of a lead trainer, which led me to cities around the United States to train scribes for work in emergency rooms.

To date, I have worked in over eleven different emergency departments, with more than eighty physicians. Every day poses new challenges for the doctors and, by proxy, the scribes, in figuring out how to streamline high-quality care. I have seen a range of pathology from common colds to multisystem trauma and watched physicians, nurses, and ancillary staff work together to help people surmount the gravest of illnesses. I appreciated that, as with research, it took strength, courage, curiosity, empathy, leadership, and determination to be a great physician. The experience inspired me to pursue a career as a physician, from my foundation as a chemist and student leader.

In the past months, my experience as a scribe made me certain that I want to participate directly in patient care, though I still hold a strong allegiance to my research career. Physicians serve their communities directly by helping the sick improve the quality of their lives through diagnosis and treatment, but they can also serve their communities by moving medicine forward through scientific inquiry. Moving forward, I want to be part of a medical-school community that will train me to be a stellar clinician. With a strong undergraduate medical education, I hope one day to leverage my leadership potential to help my patients both at the bedside and from behind the bench.

Comment: Applying a year after initially being turned down for his med school of choice, this student was subsequently accepted.

Student #6

I want to pursue a career in medicine because I want to be able to answer the calls for help from the people who need attention but do not receive as much as they need. I have always enjoyed and excelled in science and mathematics. In my junior year of high school, I began working as an aide at the dementia unit of a rehabilitation facility. Every single time I volunteered, I encountered restless residents who begged for more attention but did not receive enough. I felt they didn't receive what they needed because of their physical weakness and inability to communicate effectively. It was as if they were already dead to many. When I would look into their eyes, I would see restless residents who were anything but dead. They were as alive with life as any of us—they just needed the correct attention and sympathy to answer their cries for help. Hopefully, new medications will be developed to provide further advances in the care of dementia patients. Medicine knows no bounds, and that is something that captivates me. The dementia was not limited by the color of their skin or the histories of their heritage; there were Americans, Asians, African Americans, and Russians at the rehabilitation facility, all needing more help. I want to work to answer the call of all of these people, no matter their physical and mental orientation. The potential to help people of all kinds is the concept that motivates me to pursue a career in medicine. I hope that I will possess the ability to extend meaningful life for patients.

Comment: Demonstrates the desire to help others.

Student #7

I initiated my college education in the College of Engineering at Bradley University as a construction major. I realized that the complexities and intricacies of building any structure require a basic foundation in many trades. While attending school and learning about construction, I started to develop an interest in the basic sciences, so I began enrolling in related courses.

I have also had the opportunity to spend time with my father, who has been a physician for twenty-five years and has exposed me to his practice and daily routine in the field of medicine. I found that my father's practice in medicine was far more enriching than construction because it not only included applications of higher learning and education but also required skills in personal communication with both patients and colleagues. In addition, caring for people provides more challenges and opportunities to utilize problem-solving skills and motor skills and to take the most extreme responsibility in life by caring for another individual.

I believe that attending Bradley University in the School of Engineering has provided a building block for my educational advancement. In order to transition myself into a career in medicine, I recognized the need to expand my knowledge base in an assortment of science courses. I therefore enrolled at the University of Illinois to complete the required sciences for the medical prerequisites. Additionally, I have taken an EMT course, which provided me with some clinical experience and will better prepare me for a career in medicine. During that course, I learned the basics of emergency medical response. I also was able to work in emergency rooms, assisting the physicians in caring for patients. This not only provided a valuable learning opportunity but has heightened my desire to pursue a career in medicine.

The next step in accomplishing my ultimate goal of becoming a physician is to further enhance my knowledge to better prepare myself for medical school. The program at Rush University will provide a solid education in the field of biotechnology and is designed to prepare future medical students for the challenge of medical school. I would appreciate you giving me the opportunity to attend your university so I can contribute to the classroom experience and complete my education and career goals.

Comment: Touches many bases and demonstrates a solid foundation.

Student #8

I have been preparing myself academically for my future as a physician. As a physics major with an interest in health care, I have been taking courses over a very wide range of subjects. I made it my goal to try to expand my scientific knowledge as much as I could. I have been taking not only classes to fulfill requirements for my physics major but also classes in the biology and chemistry departments to help me prepare for my career in health care.

While these classes have been teaching me about how the human body works and develops, I have been gaining strong insight into critical thinking in completely different fields of study, such as math and physics. My studies in these subjects have given me the background to solve and analyze problems from a completely different point of view and will provide a broader spectrum of techniques and strategies to apply when approaching a problem.

As a physics major, I have been rewarded by taking classes with very strong problem-solving and critical-thinking backgrounds. This is one of the most important qualities/traits of a medical professional. I believe thinking critically and solving problems utilizing different strategies and techniques is crucial for a successful physician. My physics classes are very heavily based in problem-solving strategies and mathematical techniques that will allow me to better analyze a patient problem that I may encounter.

One experience that has had a lasting impact on my life was a mission trip I took with my family to Pivra, Peru. During this trip, we delivered food to needy families and helped build shelters in the urban area of Peru. This experience helped open my eyes to the poverty and poor conditions along with minimal health care that some people live through. The memory of these struggling people has given me the incentive and courage to do whatever I can to help people as much as I can. I believe a career in medicine will provide me with the opportunities to help and promote a healthy living for others. This experience has not only shaped my desire to be a physician but also sparked my study of Spanish, which is my minor and in which I am conversant. I would hope to one day provide primary care to Spanish-speaking people.

I wish to become a physician in order to help people in the best way that I can. Making a difference in people's lives is what motivates me. Providing people with health care is an invaluable benefit. As a physician, I will be able to take advantage of my abilities to solve problems critically in order to provide patients with the best possible health care available.

Comment: Good explanation as to how a background in physics can apply to medicine and caring for others.

Student #9

Emergency Medical Services brought a patient into the Saint Alexius Medical Center emergency room at 1:30 p.m. on a Thursday in May. The forty-five-year-old man recently underwent brain surgery and was suffering from postoperative seizures. Prior to his trip to the ER, doctors had been unable to control the symptoms through standard protocols, and the patient and his family were increasingly terrified with each seizure.

In the ER I witnessed one such seizure while working as a medical scribe for his emergency-room physician, Dr. F. I began working as a medical scribe a few months ago, and this was one of many difficult and complex cases that I witnessed. This case was also the most personally inspirational.

The patient was quickly stabilized by the ER team, led by Dr. F., and he could have been admitted to the hospital or sent home. Dr. F. had fulfilled his basic responsibilities of stabilizing the incoming patient, making sure that he was out of the woods in the immediate sense. However, Dr. F. did not allow fatigue and multiple additional responsibilities to deter him from further assessing the patient and the situation. He ordered a CT scan of the chest, which is not standard protocol in this case but which showed multiple bilateral pulmonary embolisms. Had he either admitted or discharged this patient after following standard ER protocols, this man could have died at any moment. Dr. F.'s decision to order an additional test very likely saved the patient's life. This case showed me how education and training, combined with commitment and compassion, can be the difference between life and death.

As a student at the University of Michigan, I knew that I wanted to be a doctor. I learned a great deal in the classroom and as a volunteer at the Ann Arbor Veterans Hospital. I have taken the last year to learn more about medicine and myself. I loved the training program that I took to get my emergency medical technician certification. I have learned a great deal about some of the unpleasant realities of the American health-care system by becoming a volunteer at Community Health Clinic, a free clinic for the uninsured in Chicago. I admired the all-volunteer medical staff at the clinic. In May I was fortunate to land a position as a medical scribe at the Saint Alexius Medical Center ER in suburban Chicago. Three weeks ago I was promoted to chief medical scribe. I love going to work every day (even at night).

As a volunteer at the free health clinic and working in an ER, my eyes have been opened to the many Americans that live without proper health care because they lack health insurance and how difficult it can be for them, for a variety of reasons, to maintain good health. I have seen patients walk into the Community Health Clinic and walk out feeling better because of the "care" in health care. I have seen the same thing in the emergency room at Saint Alexius Medical Center. Even the small amount of time that the volunteer physicians dedicate to the patients each week makes an enormous difference.

Both these Community Health Clinic physicians and Dr. F. have shown me the compassion and dedication it takes to truly help people. I look forward to following their example and providing both the health and the care in health care. This has been a rewarding journey, and I feel ready to enter medical school. I want to be a physician so I can help people feel better, live better, and live longer.

Comment: Excellent demonstration of experience as an emergency-room scribe.

Student #10

The last Saturday of every month was the day I most dreaded. It was the day of my public recital at a local nursing home. As a beginning pianist, I would nervously walk to the piano and wonder if I had practiced enough. After finishing my piece, I would exhale a sigh of relief, finally able to slide off the bench to take a bow. This was the moment when I came face-to-face with my audience, a room full of nursing-home residents seated in wheelchairs, clapping more vigorously and smiling more brightly than expected. I was surprised that my beginner's piece would command such enthusiasm. During those times, I realized my performance had personally enlivened the residents' spirits and helped them momentarily forget their physical discomfort, loneliness, or weakened wellness. My piece was a small contribution toward uplifting the residents and offering them a caring distraction. This early experience inspired me to wonder how I could better help people on an individual basis with more of my talents and efforts beyond a mere beginner's piano piece.

My inspiration to pursue medicine may have begun with these recitals but became further developed when I was introduced to a muscular-dystrophy patient. "Steven" was twenty-one years old, my age, and the disease had progressed to an advanced level. He was bedridden, extremely thin, and dependent on others for even the most basic of functions. I was struck by how this disease had taken away his ability to control his life in the simplest ways, drastically changing its conditions and outcomes. If Steven had not inherited muscular dystrophy, he would be able to stand, enjoy summer athletics, and prepare for a future career, just like I had. His family was very positive and attentive to his desires. They took every opportunity to empower Steven and give him some measure of quality in life. However, outside the room, they acted differently from the smiles, optimism, and strength I witnessed within. I can never forget the image of his family holding one another in the hallway and crying as silently as they could. As I watched, I desired to know exactly how to help Steven in order to brighten this family and give them the happiness they deserved. But I did not know what to do or say, and I felt absolutely powerless.

I observed the physician console the family members. It was apparent he had developed personal relationships with each person. As a counselor, educator, confidant, and physician, he was able to help the family precisely in the way I wanted to but was unable. He was treating Steven's condition medically, and more importantly, he was making every effort to treat the whole family's spirit. Watching their tears and anguish subside fueled my desire to have a direct role in bettering the health and lives of patients and families, just as this physician was doing. It would be an honor to be responsible for assisting a whole family and offering them support, hope, and compassion.

The memory of Steven's story is unforgettable. When learning about the molecular and genetic mechanism of muscular dystrophy, I am reminded of Steven. He has given me a connection to the disorder and the realization that my coursework offers knowledge beyond my personal fulfillment. By developing a strong science foundation, I would improve my ability to educate and treat future patients, but my interactions with Steven, the nursing-home residents, and other patients have added a further dimension to my pursuit of medicine. They have rooted my academic interests in the passion to learn on behalf of future patients and their families.

Once a young child seeking to play my best on a recital piece, I am now a young adult similarly inclined to make a difference in the lives of others. The relief I felt in this accomplishment as a child has been replaced by a desire to contribute to more far-reaching consequences, touching the health and welfare of a family. Knowing the potential a recital has to provide solace for a stranger, I am inspired to utilize my perseverance and dedication to quality in the field of medicine. My experiences have given me an intense desire to impact people's lives by utilizing my education, talents, and abilities. Having learned the deeper dimensions of infirmity and humanity, I can think of no greater service than that provided by a physician.

Comment: Very good explanation of personal experiences and desire to help others.

———

Student #11

Tears of sadness and fear flowed uncontrollably. My two-year-old daughter had been exhibiting signs of sickness for almost a week, and I soon found myself clutching my child on an examination table as her pediatrician diagnosed her with type 1 diabetes. The diagnosis petrified me. I had never had any exposure to medicine and knew very little about diabetes or its treatment. With a blood-glucose level well over seven hundred, my daughter was close to death and spent the next week in the ICU. The diagnosis that would forever alter my daughter's life would also alter mine but in a more positive way than expected.

Aside from the overwhelming emotions that went along with her diagnosis, the fascination of a world I had never before experienced began to captivate me. The equipment and environment at the hospital were amazing, and the incredible level of concern and mindful care the doctors and staff showed my daughter was astounding. The depth of compassion they exhibited, combined with the technology of modern medicine, entranced me.

I had always found science to be fascinating, even at a younger age. After conquering my first day of kindergarten, I was rewarded with a toy school bus equipped with pullback action. By bedtime, I had dismantled it to determine how the friction-driven mechanism propelled it. To my parents' chagrin, my room was always littered with toy parts and pieces. I was fascinated by learning how things worked. This curiosity would later find great satisfaction in my high-school science classes where, driven by self-discovery, I spent extra time in the labs marveling at the wonders of life. I often reflect on that time, and I cherish those early discoveries.

My daughter's diagnosis reawakened my fascination with science. While in the ICU with her that week, for the first time I began to view science as a mechanism that can bring healing and preservation. Additionally, I knew I had to rapidly learn to manage the care of my diabetic toddler, so I paid conscientious attention to the miniscule mechanics of her treatment and quickly became intimately involved in the daily tasks of her care. After being released from the hospital, my daughter's pediatrician and I developed a friendship. He could tell I was fascinated with his life as a physician, and he freely discussed it. As I listened to his patient stories and became aware of his understanding of the human body, I discreetly imagined myself as a physician. I could only imagine the fulfillment of impacting someone's life through selflessly caring for him or her in a time of medical need.

Imagining myself as a physician soon matured as I realized this event revealed a major turning point in my life. I had spent the last fifteen years building a successful home-building firm, yet with little hesitation I began making plans to walk away from that life to pursue a career in medicine. My family could see my passion as I poured myself into exploring medicine, including attending seminars and shadowing physicians. As a man of faith, I believed for the first time in my life that my pursuits aligned with my purpose. My plans to pursue medicine included beginning college for the first time in my life, and along the way, the demands of life and supporting a family forced a few college transfers and relocations. A year and a half ago, we relocated to a small rural town in Kentucky near where my wife was raised. My family and I enjoy this area very much and have built a life here. The town reminds me of the town I grew up in, and my wife's family, with deep Kentucky roots, is elated to see us finally call Kentucky home! Upon relocating to this area, I became aware of the University of Kentucky College of Medicine and have researched the school thoroughly. I sought out and shadowed a University of Kentucky College of Medicine graduate who is an amazing family physician south of Lexington. Conversations with him and my own research allow me to conclude that I have a desire to be able to call myself a University of Kentucky College of Medicine alumnus and remain in this area after my medical training. One of the local family physicians I have repeatedly shadowed stated it took her twenty years to form relationships that allow her to understand the generational dynamics in a small town. My prior career was built on relationships, and I value the relationships I have built thus far in the town I now call home. I look forward to the future of a permanent life here and the continuation and building upon of those relationships.

As I reflect on the journey of my life and pursue what is to come, I recall a George Eliot quote: "It is never too late to be what you might have been." I believe the events of my life have primed me for and channeled me to this moment and allow me to appreciate the fulfillment that I already experience in the pursuit of medicine. This pursuit has rekindled my love for science and revealed to me a deep love for academics and the unique engagement I enjoy with my peers as they recognize I have experienced something of life, yet can relate to the contemporary challenges of college. I feel my unique life experiences, desire to serve and care for others, exposure to medicine, and commitment to academics will enable me to be a positive contribution to the University of Kentucky College of Medicine program and live a life devoted to serving others!

Comment: This is a perfect example for an older student applying to be a physician serving in a rural community. One of the best I have ever seen!

APPENDIX B

AN EXAMPLE OF A REVISED PERSONAL STATEMENT

My unrelenting drive to become a physician has been ~~drastically~~ inspired by a vast array of people, experiences, and passions. Since I was very young, my parents have instilled in me a sense of awe and wonder at the incredible beauty and complexity of the human body. Their unyielding love for the human body and helping others not only drove them to become incredible physicians, but critically influenced the way they raised me. Growing up hearing my father enthusiastically speak about a rare blood disorder or hearing my mother talking about Crohn's disease was a very normal thing. This full absorption into a world dominated by scientific reasoning and clinical passion has inspired the way that I perceive the world, and has laid a solid foundation for what I hope to do for the rest of my life. My ~~premature~~ love for knowing how systems work at a fundamental level in biology, chemistry, and physics was enough for me to decide to embark on a scientific journey in college.

As I began my classes at Boston University, I was challenged by the increased complexity of my classes and ~~overwhelming~~ workload. My first year at Boston University cast doubts on whether I would be able to perform what I most loved. It was a very frustrating time that made me more resilient and more determined to study longer hours, complete supplemental coursework, and reach out to my professors when I did not understand concepts. It was not until the summer after freshman year that I had my first calling and inspiration to become a physician.

During the summer going into sophomore year, I attended an annual picnic at my father's oncology office. It was a hot, humid summer day at a large recreational field, and many families of the people who worked at the office were there. As I was eating and talking to my coworker, I noticed that she started to slur her words and stopped making any sense. At first I thought she just confused her words and I ~~joked with her,~~ asked what she meant by what she had just said. ~~As a few seconds proceeded,~~ After a few seconds, I was immediately alerted that she was unable to speak and became unresponsive. In an instant of ~~intense~~ fear for my coworker's health, I immediately sprinted across the field to get the attention of my father and his coworkers and told them what had just happened. It was their reaction to my crucial information that established my drive to become a physician, and my belief that it was my destiny. As they called for paramedics, they immediately knew to check for vitals, positioned her legs upward, and performed several physiological tests. The ability of these physicians to immediately respond at this critical stage and recognize what physiological systems might be impacted and act~~ing~~ accordingly to potentially save the girl's life made me realize what I wanted to do with my ~~intense~~ passion for science—it was ~~my fate~~ to become a physician.

As I continued with the rest of my college career as a biology and psychology major, I began taking higher-level classes that built on the fundamentals I had previously learned. My renewed vigor to better understand processes in the human body so that I could one day help those in need enabled me to begin excelling in my classes. Taking classes that ~~intricately~~ taught me the foundation of physiological systems such as the endocrine, respiratory, and circulatory systems gave me a ~~euphoric~~ yearning to learn more. My ~~once frustrating~~ classes became fundamental steps to understanding and ~~reciprocally~~ appreciating the wonders of the human body.

Although the beauty and complexity of the human body inspires me to study science and participate in research, it is my passion to help those in need that drives me toward medicine. Although I have worked in underprivileged communities and have volunteered to assist others my entire life, as a physician I will have the tools to help those most in need. My ability to provide hope, care, and empathy to underprivileged communities will be my priority ~~and greatest glamor~~. My compassion would allow me to sincerely relate with the patient, allowing us to work together toward successful treatment. My ~~instinctive~~ passion to help those in need has heightened my desire to be a physician.

As a physician, my ~~insatiable~~ thirst ~~for knowing~~ to know more about the extraordinarily complex human body would drive me to perform research and help those in need. I expect to learn medicine by researching the human brain, the enigmatic organ that most intrigues me. With my background in psychology, I believe I can integrate my love of biological systems with my ~~intense~~ interest ~~of~~ in the human brain. By better understanding the localized integrated functions of the human brain, I can further help recognize the causes of brain disorders and related phenomena. The importance of the human brain in controlling the physiological functions of the human body is unquestioned, and the knowledge of how it works is still very limited. I expect to research many of these unanswered questions and develop treatments to better the lifestyles of those with brain defects. This unyielding drive to unlock the remaining mysteries of the human body while helping better the lives of others will ~~not only~~ undoubtedly fulfill not only my role as a physician but as a person as well.

APPENDIX C

HYPOTHETICAL WRITTEN RESPONSES TO SPECIFIC QUESTIONS FOR ADMISSION TO A MEDICAL SCHOOL IN A STUDENT'S SOPHOMORE YEAR OF COLLEGE

- What honors did you receive while in high school / college?

AP Scholar with Distinction Award
Illinois State Scholar
Prairie State Achievement Award for Math and Science
National Honor Society member
Spanish Honor Society member
Carl Sandburg High School Honor Roll (eight semesters)
Saint Xavier University Dean's List
Sheriff's Youth Service Medal of Honor
President's Volunteer Service Award
Mid-Suburban League All-Academic Senior Athlete Award
Carl Sandburg High School Athletic Wall of Fame (four years)
Sportsmanship Award from Chicago District Tennis Association (2007)
Ranked #1 in doubles in Chicago District Tennis Association (2008)

- In what extracurricular, community, and/or vocational activities have you participated while in high school / college?

High-school varsity tennis team (Second doubles each year and state qualifier each year. My team finished sixth in state my freshman and sophomore years and finished fourth in state my junior and senior years.)
High-school student ambassador (2008)
Volunteer at Saint Alexius Medical Center (2006–2010)
Saint Xavier University Tennis Team (#1 singles and #1 doubles)
Saint Xavier University Pre-Health Club (public relations cochairman)
Saint Xavier University Habitat for Humanity
Saint Xavier University Intramural Basketball
Kappa Kappa Gamma (recording and corresponding secretary)

- If you have been employed during the regular school year while in high school /
college, specify the type of work and approximate hours per week, currently and
previous to this year.

During my sophomore year of high school, I worked for the park district as both a lifeguard and
a swim instructor for approximately ten hours per week. Throughout my junior and senior years
of high school, I worked as a transporter for the Radiology Department at Saint Alexius Medical
Center for approximately sixteen hours per week. As a transporter, I brought the inpatients from
their rooms down to the Radiology Department, where they would get x-rays, an MRI, a CT
scan, an ultrasound, and so on. In addition to my position as a transporter, while I was a senior
in high school, I worked as a medical assistant for Northwest Health Care for four hours each
week. In this position, I prepared patients for the physician. I would bring a patient to a room,
take his or her vitals, and discuss with the patient the reason for his or her visit and the medications he or she was currently taking. I would then record this information in the patient's chart
for the physician to reference.

- How have you spent your summers during high school?

During the summer of 2006, I volunteered in Piura, Peru. My volunteer work consisted of hous-
ing construction, food and clothing delivery, teaching English to children, and volunteering at
an orphanage. During the summer of 2007, I attended health class in summer school. During
the summer of 2008, I worked full-time as a lifeguard and swim instructor. I also did volunteer
work in Costa Rica with Rustic Pathways. Rustic Pathways is a youth volunteer program that
offers high-school students the opportunity to travel to one of many different countries and
partake in community-service projects. During my volunteer time in Costa Rica, I did construction work for environmental projects. I painted and constructed fences for a local elementary
school, as well as taught English to children and families. I also built hatcheries and participated
in night walks to protect turtle eggs from predators.

During the summer of 2009, I worked approximately forty hours per week at Saint Alexius
Medical Center as a transporter for the Radiology Department. During the summer of 2010, I
had an unpaid internship at the University of Illinois College of Pharmacy, which was designed
to introduce students to the field of clinical research.

I shadowed a physician while she saw patients in an epilepsy clinic, aided in editing a textbook,
and attended Toxicon. (Toxicon is a consortium of medical students, residents, and fellows

from emergency departments and pediatrics. At the Toxicon meetings, we discussed the cases of patients who entered Illinois hospitals due to toxic ingestions.) I also took part in a journal club and learned about the grant application process, IRB (Institutional Review Board), and OPRS (Office for the Protection of Research Subjects). I also worked about sixteen hours per week as a transporter. There was also a two-week period during that summer when I traveled to Seville, Spain, with a group of students from my high school. While in Spain, I attended class every day to learn about the language and the culture. We also went on tours around the city and learned about the history of many historical sites. In addition, every summer throughout high school, I volunteered at Saint Alexius Medical Center for four hours each week. Also, I played tennis two hours per day, at least five days per week, each summer.

- What do you feel is your greatest academic strength? Explain.

I think my greatest academic strength is that I tend to grasp new material quickly, especially math and science classes, because I am good at conceptualizing. This year during winter term, I took calculus; every day I needed to use my problem-solving skills. For example, I was trying to find the distance between a point and a plane in three-dimensional space. It is easy for me to picture this and realize that I need to solve this problem by finding the vector that both contains the given point and is perpendicular to the plane. I am able to analyze the big picture, figure out what I need to do, and use what I have been taught to solve the problem. I am capable of looking through a chapter and grasping the concepts in one night. However, knowing the concepts only allows me to begin the problem. Time and experience have taught me that grasping concepts quickly puts me in between not having any information and having enough knowledge to be able to solve the problems.

Even though I understand the problems and how to begin them, I do need to put forth time and effort solving many practice problems to thoroughly master new material. I have come to realize that once I figure out how to address one type of problem, my curiosity intrigues me to learn the next concept, meaning I take pleasure in the pursuit of more information. Also, due to the fact that I have been more inclined toward the sciences, I decided to go against what is considered the normal track of my high school. Ordinarily, students would take biology as freshmen, honors chemistry as sophomores, honors physics as juniors, and then AP Biology, AP Chemistry, or AP Physics as seniors. However, I decided to challenge myself by skipping honors physics in order to take AP Biology as a junior and AP Physics as a senior. I felt that this switch would be important in order to best prepare myself for college and to challenge myself academically.

- What do you feel is your greatest nonacademic strength? Explain.

I feel my greatest nonacademic strength is that I am morally and ethically strong. I grew up in a home where two different religions are observed, and while this could have been confusing for me, I found it to be extremely educational. I was able to see how the two religions are practiced and how, even though there were differences, both of the religions were based on truth, honesty, and kindness. It has been instilled in me to treat individuals with kindness, and I have been raised with the moral code of treating others the way that I would want to be treated. Today, I find that I am interested in people's differences, probably because of the way I was raised.

- What do you feel is your greatest academic weakness? Explain.

While I love to read, my greatest academic weakness is my reading speed. When I read, I sub-vocalize, to use the term that was taught to me. This means that I say each word in my mind while reading, thus slowing me down and making reading a sometimes frustrating task. To change this habit, during this upcoming term, I am taking an independent study with the director of Saint Xavier University's Center for Teaching and Learning. The director is the person who taught me about subvocalizing, and he has worked with many students to improve their reading. During this course, I will learn to increase my reading speed as well as to improve my comprehension. I recognize that medical school requires a tremendous amount of reading, and I believe this course will prove to be very useful to me.

- What do you feel is your greatest nonacademic weakness? Explain.

I tend to be a little cautious when I first meet people. I want to avoid saying things that might cause people to misread me, which leads me to being less talkative than I might be when I encounter a new acquaintance. Although I become much more self-aware and careful with what I say, I also become more observant with my listening skills when I am in these situations. My cautiousness allows me to avoid jumping to assumptions, but it can inhibit spontaneous interaction. I like to think that my being cautious explains why I work well with teams or groups. Because there is less focus on me, I can contribute without the pressure of leading the group. I am confident that I will improve on this weakness with time and practice and with the confidence that comes from taking my medical training seriously. I have already attempted to improve this weakness by choosing a job that was outside my comfort zone. In this position, in order to comfort others, I was forced to be more outgoing with fellow employees and patients; it certainly increased my self-confidence in starting conversations with people I do not know.

- Who do you feel will be most likely to provide you emotional support while in college and medical school? Explain your relationship with and your reason for choosing this person or persons.

My mother and my father will provide me with support throughout undergraduate school and medical school. They have always been there to support me in everything that I have wanted to accomplish. They taught me the morals and values that I live my life by. Because of them, I work hard and respect, help, and care about others. Due to the fact that they both attended college in the medical field, they will be able to help me adjust to the differences between medical school and undergraduate school; they will provide me with support through their experiences.

- List your hobbies in order of importance to you.

My hobbies include tennis, snow skiing, snowboarding, playing chess, reading, water skiing, and playing leisure sports such as basketball, volleyball, and golf. I enjoy physically demanding activities that allow me to relieve stress and unwind from mentally strenuous activities during school.

- State one major problem you encountered during the last three years and explain how you dealt with it.

I have been extremely fortunate throughout my life in that I have not encountered very many large problems. However, I was challenged during my first trimester of college when I had to deal with the passing of my grandfather. It was my first time living away from home, and I found it to be very difficult to deal with my loss especially because I was far away from my family. Although I was able to go home for a few days to grieve with my family, the pain had not subsided upon my return to Saint Xavier University. I recognized that this was not a problem that I could resolve on my own, so I took it upon myself to use the resources available at Saint Xavier such as counselors, friends, and my RA in order to find support during such a hard time. Witnessing my father's pain made me realize that the most important thing for me to do at that time was to be there for him. Upon my return to school, I called him every day to let him know that he was not alone during this tragedy. This situation was particularly difficult because it occurred a week before finals. I had to reorganize myself and use my time-management skills in order to give myself time to grieve, call my family, and study for finals.

- How do you feel that Michigan State Medical School can contribute to your growth and development as a professional in the field of medicine?

Because Michigan State is a very close community, I feel that I will be encouraged to learn the sciences and skills that are necessary for a physician. I also will be taught how to apply my integrity for the patient's benefit. Michigan State offers individual attention from faculty. I have had the opportunity to speak to several physicians regarding the medical schools they attended. Some have referred to their experiences as "assembly line" training where they were just a "number" or "statistic" in their medical class. This is not the medical education experience that I am interested in. Several Michigan State students, including my brother, stated that this was not their experience. They tell me that they have been given an outstanding individual education. They learned from teachers and preceptors who treated them with respect and who did not patronize them; their instructors were available and approachable. My brother felt his training at Michigan State led him to score extremely high on his step 1 exam and led him to receive the AOA award. I am confident that Michigan State Medical School will provide me with a quality medical education.

Michigan State University Medical Center has an outstanding reputation. As you know, in the 2010 *US News & World Report*'s issue on "America's Best Hospitals," Michigan State was ranked in the top fifty in several specialties. It has recently opened a new orthopedic building where the physicians have become nationally known for their minimally invasive orthopedic surgeries. The new outpatient cancer center has become an example for combining patient comforts with state-of-the-art medical technology. The new Michigan State Hospital is scheduled to open in 2012 and is going to be a leader in the newest advances in medical care. I would feel honored to be a part of this growing medical network.

I will be able to gain the ability to fulfill a physician's responsibility to a patient with competence and compassion. Sustainability at Michigan State is something that is very important to me. Because Michigan State is known for being well-rounded in all specialties, I will be able to explore all of my options in order to choose what specialty I would like to pursue. I will also have the opportunity to experience a wide variety of specialties during my third-year and fourth-year rotations in order to learn what field of medicine I want to pursue. Michigan State's hospital network will give me the opportunities a medical student needs to grow and develop.

I plan on continuing to be involved in community service while I attend medical school. The Michigan State Community Service Initiative Program (MSCSIP) that is offered will allow me to continue performing community service. For example, I would like to be involved with the Buddies Program. I would love to have the opportunity to mentor a chronically ill child, which would be a very rewarding experience for me. Another community-service program that Michigan State offers that particularly interests me is the MammoVan Program, through which I can help educate an underserved population about women's health issues. Due to a combination of all of the above, I feel Michigan State Medical School will provide me with the education, support, and growth needed in the field of medicine.

- Briefly describe your personal characteristics that make you effective in working with people and outline your skills, interests, aptitude, and temperament in relation to your suitability for a career in medicine.

Honesty, hopefulness, patience, empathy, and hard work are a few of my characteristics that make me effective in working with people. My honesty will help me deal with individuals facing illness. Patients value honesty in health-care providers. My parents have always instilled in me the importance of being honest, and this characteristic will support the interaction I will have with others. I like to think that I am not only honest with others but also honest with myself. I understand that I, like everyone else, have room for improvement; I could be more self-confident and more knowledgeable about things like politics and world issues. I know that medical school will be tough and require a tremendous amount of time and effort. There will be many challenges that I will need to overcome, but I am prepared to face these challenges.

It is important to balance honesty that with hope. I am confident that as I gain more experience in caring for patients, I can provide a balance of hope and honesty about their disease.

I have tremendous patience. Being the youngest in my family with three older brothers has given me the ability to live through stressful situations and still remain patient. I have always shown empathy for others. During my volunteer experience in Peru, I felt the daily struggles of the people both medically and financially. It was during this time that my desire to become a physician and someday return to Peru to provide medical care was reinforced.

I am hardworking. Whether it be in academics, employment, or athletics, I have always put 100 percent into whatever I endeavor. For example, my senior year of high school I took AP Physics, which is normally taken after honors physics. Even though I had taken no prior physics class, I was confident that I could succeed in this course because I was willing to put in the extra effort that was required in order to receive a better education. I feel all of these qualities will benefit me as I pursue a career in medicine.

- What other career possibilities have you considered, and why have you rejected them?

Because I enjoy science and math, I looked at possibilities within these two areas. Taking into account that I want a career that is mentally stimulating and personally rewarding, the two choices that I was most seriously considering were engineer and physician. However, I believe that a career as a physician would be much more personally rewarding because I would have the privilege to help and to make a difference in the lives of others on an almost daily basis.

- Briefly describe your experiences in working with people, the general responsibilities of each, and how long you held the position. If you have had limited experiences in working with people in the health field, be sure to list any life experiences, both paid or voluntary, including in high school, college, or community service.

For the four years that I volunteered at the hospital, I had the responsibilities of completing the discharge of patients and escorting outpatients to the Radiology Department. Although the likelihood of a problem occurring was fairly small, we were still required to know how to handle a situation if a problem occurred. For example, I escorted a patient who was extremely combative to the point where I needed to ask for a code to be called. When I called the code, security arrived quickly and helped me take the patient back to his room, where we were able to calm him down. In that small moment, I was responsible for the patient's safety and for the safety of everyone around him. It wasn't until later that I realized that we are all called upon to serve in such capacities, large and small. During my sophomore year and the following summer, I worked as a lifeguard and a swim instructor. I worked with other lifeguards, club members, and children taking swim lessons. I was responsible for the safety of everyone in and around the pool and was trained in CPR and first aid. Eventually, I left this position in order to pursue my job as a hospital transporter.

As a transporter, I learned how to handle different situations: projectile vomiting, incontinence, cardiac arrest, uncomfortable patients, and overly involved family members, to name a few. I maintained this position while also working as a medical assistant at a physician's office during my senior year. I had the responsibility of bringing patients to the examining room and preparing them for the physician. For this position, I was trained in taking vitals, performing finger-stick glucose tests, and performing urinalyses. I had to recognize if the patients needed tests to be performed in office before the physician met with them. For example, if the patient was suffering from back pain and had no explanation for that pain, then I recognized that I should perform a urinalysis before the physician met with the patient.

• What plans do you have following graduation from medical school?

At this point in time, I am unsure of which field of medicine I plan on pursuing. I do want to go into a field that emphasizes the patient-physician relationship because I love working with people, and I have loved interacting with many patients while volunteering and working at a hospital. I would like to practice in the Chicago area. However, while I was doing volunteer work in Piura, Peru, there was a nurse who would attend to the ill, and physicians would only come about once a month from the larger cities nearby. After witnessing this lack of good health care, I would like to spend some time, perhaps several weeks each year, practicing in an impoverished area of the world similar to Piura. Overall, I am staying open-minded and am excited to explore many different options that the study of medicine offers.

• *For Personal Comments. (Use this space or attach a sheet explaining the basis of your decision to become a physician and also to describe how your receiving an early Michigan State admission commitment would affect your undergraduate program.)*

My decision to become a physician has been a progressive process. At a young age, I had been most interested in science class. This interest developed as I became more and more curious about the science behind everything, whether it is how molecules interact or how the human body works. Due to the fact that medicine and medical practice are always evolving, I think being a physician will give me the privilege to continuously learn new things. It will be intellectually demanding every day, which is something I look for in a profession.

Upon entering high school, I decided that volunteering at a hospital would help me to decide whether or not being a physician would be a career that I would want to pursue. Being exposed to different aspects of health care only sparked my interest further. I then decided to apply for a position as a transporter for the Radiology Department. My interaction with numerous patients with a wide variety of different diagnoses made me determined to pursue a job within the medical field.

My participation in the internship at the University of Illinois College of Pharmacy has sparked my interest in research. I am hoping that an early admission to Michigan State Medical School will allow me to be involved in an extended research project and, perhaps, to study abroad, maybe in Denmark, where they practice socialized medicine.

Volunteer work and helping others is very important to me. It has always been something that I thoroughly enjoy. I first realized how rewarding it is to assist others when I went to Piura, Peru, and had the opportunity to make a difference in the lives of those living without running water in homes made of burlap sacks. Ever since that experience, I have continued to volunteer. I volunteered at a hospital every week. I did construction work in Costa Rica. I became a member of Habitat for Humanity. I also organize bingo at a nursing home every Christmas Eve. My compassion and desire to help others led me to my volunteer work. Being a physician will allow me to help others in the most intimate of ways, how they experience themselves and their health.

If I were to have the advantage of an early Michigan State admission commitment, it would allow me to experience the fullness of the Saint Xavier curriculum, conduct research, and perhaps even travel abroad.

Comment: This student did an excellent job of responding to all questions.

APPENDIX D

ONE STUDENT'S PREPARATION FOR MEDICAL SCHOOL

1. Describe a valuable experience in your personal development. This might be a decision you have made, an achievement of which you are particularly proud of, or a person who has influenced your life.

I am a poor-to-middling public speaker. I'm not nervous; I'm just not good at it. However, around last January, the National Collegiate EMS Foundation put out an advertisement for a competition in which a collegiate EMT would give an hour-long academic lecture on a topic relevant to collegiate EMS. I am a member of MIT EMS, and at the time I had recently run a call alongside a city ambulance. I was struck by the fact that my service had to, and did, provide the same level of care to our patients as the city's service, while being exposed to a significantly lower variety of calls. I decided to make a presentation based on how our service coped with the challenge where our most experienced EMT had all of three and a half years of time treating patients, and the best practices that we had adapted as a result. I prepared a proposal, requested feedback and edits from my fellow EMTs, and sent it in. I ended up being picked as a finalist, one of six chosen to give a talk at the conference that would count for continuing-education credit. Realizing that I needed to rehearse if I was to have any chance at being successful, I sent out a request to my service for volunteers to evaluate a dress rehearsal. Around ten of my fellow EMTs showed up, and their feedback was brutal. My slides were poorly designed, concepts were explained poorly, and my speech was too rapid. I made some changes and, a week later, invited them to a second rehearsal. Once again, deficiencies were pointed out: my posture was poor, hand gestures were odd, and verbal tics were obvious. But I was told that I had at least gotten better. While it was hardly perfect, I'm proud of the effort I put in and the final result.

2. Provide in detail an experience of working with individuals from diverse backgrounds. What was the experience? How did it have an impact on you?

I grew up in a suburban bubble, and my friends' parents were almost exclusively college-educated professionals. Before I came to college, I had never seen anyone underage drink alcohol or smoke a cigarette, let alone use illegal drugs. In my mind, drug use was something criminals and "other" people did, and a person who smoked was automatically worthy of contempt for his or her idiocy. Then I came to college. Most others shared my view on cigarette and drug use, but a minority did not, and many of my fellow students in my dorm regularly smoked cigarettes and used marijuana. Initially, I held them all in contempt and avoided studying or working on homework together with them. Then I slowly realized that when they weren't smoking or drinking, they were actually fine people. My impression slowly started to change. One night, I finally asked one avid smoker named Nate why he didn't quit, and his answer was astonishingly simple: It was his choice. He knew the risks and even had a grandparent with COPD. But it was how he'd been raised. He was set on joining the marines, figured he "wouldn't live forever anyway," and decided that this would be his vice, just as it had been his father's. I argued ferociously with him but finally came to accept his choice. Much else about him was foreign to me: While we worked on homework, he'd frequently take small breaks every hour or so to randomly play videogames or otherwise have fun, before getting back on task. As an eighteen-year-old freshman, he'd frequently get smashed. And of course, his style of speaking was distinctly slow, southern, and backwater. But I rapidly appreciated his intelligence and outlook. By sophomore year, we were helping each other pass test after test and have become great friends. Since then I've been exposed to hundreds of smokers and alcohol abusers through my work in primary care and in EMS, and my contempt has changed to something closer to understanding. Still, meeting and working with Nate was critical to my change in attitude toward a great swath of people I would have previously dismissed out of hand.

3. What do you hope to contribute to the field of medicine? And what do you hope to get out of a career in medicine?

I would like to become an academic physician, carrying out research in health-care organization, health-care delivery, or medical devices, in addition to maintaining an active clinical practice. Further on in my career, I would hope to take more of a leadership role in managing a hospital or working in the Public Health Service or similar organization. As an engineer, my job and predilection is to fix things, whether they be machines, organizations, or people's bodies. I would like to contribute to the field of medicine by helping to improve all of the above: developing better medical devices, establishing organizations that deliver better care, and directly taking care of patients.

In terms of what I hope to get out of medicine, I am still inspired by figures such as Dr. W., Dr. E., and Dr. K. All three are over one hundred years old, still seeing patients, and claim they'll never retire. All of them have the same advice: love what you do. I see medicine as a field that I can love. Work will hopefully never feel like work, because every day I'll be looking forward to doing what I do. In medicine, there are opportunities to exercise leadership and to work on one's own, to creatively think up new solutions and to apply learned skills with discipline and precision, and to be caring and compassionate but also to display calm and dispassion under pressure. In short, medicine offers a chance for a varied and fulfilling professional life, one that I hope I will never tire of.

Northwestern: I cannot express how much I am looking forward to Northwestern's PBL curriculum and how well it will fit my learning style. My personality's fit for Northwestern comes through best in my performance in a class called Microcomputer Project Lab. When I started, I had the barest conception of what a microcontroller was—I only knew from the rumor mill that the class was hard but rewarding and that it fulfilled a requirement. The professor didn't really teach us all that much. Instead, he provided us with chips, wire, and electromechanical equipment and assigned large but clearly defined tasks. The only way we learned was by reading technical manuals and figuring out on our own how to put it all together. I ended up building a very rudimentary x-ray-like sensor, a telephone dialer, and various other devices from scratch. I loved it, both for the knowledge I gained and the collegial atmosphere. Many of my fellow students and I regularly worked till the lab closed at 11:45 p.m. figuring out how to design and build the devices. We'd curse, commiserate, order pizza, and help each other fix whatever wasn't working. By the end of the class, I had to come up with an independent final project. My grade was set, but I decided I wanted to end with a bang. I researched ACLS protocols, learned a few aluminum machining techniques, and refreshed my knowledge of kinematics. The result was a rudimentary ACLS simulator, with a physical "beating heart." This experience is just one example of how I much prefer classes that allow me to learn on my own.

More generally, I am constantly seeking knowledge on my own. I used to read the newspaper cover to cover and now peruse CNN instead. I've even tried to improve my skills as an EMT-Basic outside of any formal curriculum. I've learned from several YouTube lectures created for the Northwestern University Rotating Resident Curriculum and audited an ATLS course at the Boston Medical Center. I also love to teach and pass on this knowledge to my fellow EMTs. Finally, if it isn't evident in all of the above, let me say it again—I cannot describe how excited and prepared I am for Northwestern's curriculum.

I use a wide variety of coping strategies to deal with stressful situations, and I feel in general that I am well prepared for the stress of medical school. I cannot express how much I am looking forward to Northwestern's PBL curriculum and how well it will fit my learning style. But I think my personal characteristics and how they'll help me at Feinberg will be evident in a story.

When I first joined MIT EMS, I found that many of the older EMTs subscribed to an old philosophy about training rookies: mistakes should be instantly and severely criticized. This was my first real exposure to such vicious criticism, and initially my confidence was severely shaken. On one call, I couldn't take a patient's blood pressure while we bounced along in the back of an ambulance with the sirens screaming en route to the hospital. The resulting dressing down after dropping off the patient lasted ten minutes, took place in front of my peers, and was utterly humiliating. However, I endured and soon began to rationalize the criticism: at least I was told exactly what I was doing wrong. It was a direct feedback loop: the harsher the criticism, the faster I would improve. And so I did—my confidence recovered with my new perspective, and my skills rapidly progressed. Now, I am the one responsible for teaching new EMTs. While I don't subscribe at all to the philosophy of subjecting people to the yelling and humiliation that I was subjected to, I still directly tell my juniors exactly what they are doing wrong.

Also, while I hate to rely on others, I have come to recognize that friends and colleagues are an invaluable resource. When I first started MIT and was faced with a confluence of several tests and projects, I would try to tough it out. Projects in which I was working with a team would take priority, followed by the subjects I was weakest in. All my activities would continue as normal. I distinctly recall leading my fraternity brothers in bailing out our flooded kitchen for two hours when I had an economics exam and major statistics project due the next day. However, as I was loaded with heavier responsibilities and harder courses, I slowly began to rely on my friends when I truly needed to. I found my fellow EMTs were more than happy to cover my shifts, as I would do when they faced crunch times. My fraternity brothers gladly helped me study for an exam in a class they had taken last year. My academics in general became a little easier once I learned to ask for help when I needed it.

My summer job in a solo primary-care practice was probably the single largest impulse for me to become a doctor. I was exposed to the front lines of medicine in a way I had never previously been—my work as an EMT on a college campus didn't compare at all. I also had a terrific mentor in Dr. B., whom I worked for. I met an incredible variety of people, all with fascinating and saddening stories: a father and owner of a small business too embarrassed to tell his children he was incontinent due to rectal cancer; a thirty-year veteran teacher with hypertension, hypercholesterolemia, and diabetes in total denial that she needed any medication; a lonely eighty-year-old with no one left after his wife, who was also our patient, passed away. I couldn't imagine how they all mustered the strength to get through the day. I would frequently get to them first to take vitals and a history, and they'd perk up a bit, glad to finally be seen. But they lit up when Dr. B. walked in. She would greet each and every one with a smile, ask about their lives, and then proceed to put to rest their concerns. She would rapidly diagnose any new problems and had a literal encyclopedia of tests, drugs, and dosages in her head and knew which ones were covered by which insurance to boot. Even when she could do nothing but talk, she would. I saw her spend an hour trying to convince a lonely elderly woman whose husband had just died to go to therapy. She eventually did and came back a month and a half later with her face and hair all made up—I almost didn't recognize her. Our patients struggled with pain or depression and were seen an hour late or more, but almost all left feeling a little happier and a little better after Dr. B. talked with them. Throughout the summer, I saw firsthand the incredible power to do good that a doctor wields. Even the patients with debilitating diseases that we could do little for—paraplegics, a poorly compliant schizophrenic, and others—left her office smiling and saying "thank you." The experience revealed how much good I could do if I dedicated my life to the practice of medicine and how rewarding it could be.

Stanford: The Stanford curriculum's scholarly concentration will help me develop my background in engineering and use it to find solutions to health-care problems. I have heard from several current residents that, during medical school, they became focused on exams and grades and lost sight of what they'd hoped to do when they first entered medical school. However, with Stanford's requirement of a scholarly concentration, there is a clear path and stimulus to stay focused on my goals. In particular, the bioengineering, health services and policy research, and medical education foundation areas all align with my interests, and the global health application area is also appealing. These areas can all serve as conduits through which I can gain experience in applying my engineering skills to medicine.

While an Indian American male from an upper-middle-class background is hardly a rare sight on a medical-school campus, the perspective I bring as an engineer sets me apart. In particular, as an aerospace engineer, I have had training in large-team organization and human-machine interaction. In terms of the former, my department's capstone course throws its entire graduating class to work on a real-world project to design and build a satellite or small air vehicle from scratch, forcing a group of thirtyish people to organize and function like a company. In terms of the latter, MIT's curriculum emphasizes making machines easy and intuitive to use. For example, in my aerospace biomedical class, it was pointed out that a space suit that doesn't remind a spacewalking astronaut which button increases the air-conditioning and which shuts off the oxygen supply will lead to very unhappy (and very dead) astronauts. This is a nontrivial problem when all these buttons are mounted on the suit's torso and the astronaut can't look down because the helmet is rigidly attached to said torso. The same principle is relevant to the design of anesthesia machines, where it should be very hard to turn the flow of oxygen down to zero and very easy to tell what button does what. These experiences will allow me to evaluate and conduct research on medical organizations and medical-machine user interfaces, as well as bring a different mind-set to a variety of problems. I have also clocked over one thousand hours as an EMT. I worked in a collegiate EMS organization where in two years one becomes one of the most senior members, and my duties now include teaching the new EMTs. Thus, I have had the heavy responsibility of teaching others skills that they must know to properly care for other people's lives. This burden has given me a new insight into what my instructors did to train me and will serve me well in medical school, residency, and beyond.

Georgetown: Why Georgetown, and what will it do for my career? First, I was pleasantly surprised to learn from the website that Georgetown has made the ownership of a handheld smartphone mandatory and has integrated it into the curriculum. As an engineer, I know very well that the use of software in critical tasks has made many services safer and more efficient. Even the great piloting of Captain Chesley Sullenberger, who glided his plane into the Hudson River, was helped by the plane's software-based controls, which let him fly without worrying that his aircraft was about to fall out of the sky. Similarly, computer-based tools can frequently help deliver medical care with fewer errors and greater speed, and Georgetown clearly recognizes this with its curriculum. I hope to learn from and contribute to such an environment, one that clearly encourages the use of the latest technology to improve medical education and the delivery of care.

Secondly, I am looking forward to a curriculum that formally covers the intangibles of a career in medicine. Even as an EMT on a college service, I have seen fellow students sucked into working on the ambulance, with both their grades and eventually their patient care compromised as a result. Others became extremely technically competent but never displayed much empathy to their patients. (Though MIT EMS tries to weed out those who became EMTs for the adrenaline rush of driving with lights and sirens screaming, we are about as successful at it as medicine has been at controlling costs.) The seventeen objectives / desired competencies of Georgetown are a good way to stay focused on the fact that being a doctor takes more than the simple memorization of factoids regarding the human body. This will be invaluable throughout medical school and during my actual career, when the intangibles will come fully into play.

Thirdly, I find Georgetown's location quite attractive. Being in Washington, DC, is an incredible advantage. Health care's future in America will literally be decided less than an hour away from campus. It may be naive to hope that a medical-school student can contribute to a process hijacked by several hundred million dollars' worth of lobbying. Nevertheless, the experience should still prove invaluable to my understanding of where my profession will go in the future.

Finally, Georgetown's emphasis on service resonates strongly with me. The community-service requirement provides a conduit to accomplishing something I hoped to do in medical school regardless: use my skills and knowledge as I develop them to help those who are not nearly as fortunate as me.

Thank you for considering me for the Georgetown School of Medicine Class of 2016.

Columbia: One strong appeal of P&S is the School of Engineering and Applied Sciences at Columbia University. My current research into designing an orthotic to correct drop foot and other neurological disorders is at the intersection of medicine and engineering, and I look forward to working with the world-class engineers at SEAS on interdisciplinary projects and research while in medical school. Another appeal is Columbia's location: an urban area with a diverse patient population. Indeed, I was very excited to hear about the CoSMO and CHHMP programs, through which I can make a positive impact and gain valuable clinical exposure to a variety of diseases. Finally, Columbia's P&S club and the strong student community it supports are quite attractive.

I would like to comment on two aspects of my application.

First, my engineering curriculum: My degree says aerospace engineering with information technology, but my exposure has been quite broad. In fact, up till junior year, I was on a track to double major in aerospace engineering and electrical engineering with computer science. I've taken courses in systems engineering, computation structures, software engineering, and microcontroller system design. The last course mentioned is a capstone engineering course for the Electrical Engineering / Computer Science Department. For my solo final project in that class, I researched basic cardiology and then used my woodworking, machining, and coding skills to create a rudimentary ACLS simulator with a physically "beating" heart, powered by four motors. The system would simulate rhythms such as ventricular fibrillation, and then respond to the correct intervention, as selected on a keypad, by going into normal sinus rhythm.

Secondly, my work as an EMT with MIT Emergency Medical Services included a large variety of opportunities. I audited an ATLS course at the Boston Medical Center as a patient, taught and mentored many junior EMTs, and attended the National Collegiate EMS Foundation's national conference. Before the conference, I applied for a speaking slot as part of a student-speaker competition and was selected as one of six finalists. I gave a lecture to around fifty other collegiate EMTs from around the nation on how best to prepare and train for certain calls, such as cardiac arrests that are relatively rare on a college campus.

Currently, along with a graduate-student supervisor, I have been researching orthotics for the correction of drop foot via the use of functional electrical stimulation. The technique we have been investigating is the use of surface electrodes located near the knee that stimulate the peroneal nerve, which innervates the tibialis anterior muscle. We then record the foot's resultant lift using inertial measurement units (IMUs) strapped onto the foot and shin. Over the course of my work, I have independently run subjects through trials; modified our experimental protocol; applied for a protocol modification from MIT's COUHES (Committee on the Use of Humans as Experimental Subjects); modified the Simulink software model we are using to control our stimulators; and, along with my supervisor, analyzed our data to develop a model that can predict the response of the tibialis anterior muscle to electrical stimulation across multiple subjects. We have just started to collect data, but we look forward to sending a paper for publication within the next year or so.

How I'd react to a situation where someone wasn't pulling their weight would depend a lot on the time frame. If the time period is short and urgent, I'd just take up the slack myself. For example, I work on an ambulance service that typically runs three-person crews. When one of my teammates applied a splint that didn't stabilize the limb or didn't perform a rapid and thorough interview, I'd immediately take over and do things properly. Afterward, I'd go over what went wrong and how that member of my team could do better. Similarly, if the group's deliverable was due the next day or so, I would do the extra work myself or jointly with another group member.

On the other hand, if the group had a longer deadline for its work, I'd take aside the group member and start a conversation. In my experience, few people are simply lazy or uncaring about a small group's objectives. Instead, they typically have other commitments or personal situations that prevent them from focusing on their work. Consequently, I'd offer to help them resolve their personal situation or get the group to take some of the load off of their shoulders while they resolve their (hopefully) temporary predicament.

Yale: There are literally one hundred reasons why I want to attend Yale for my medical education. But more important is what I can contribute to Yale's incredible environment and how Yale can help me achieve my career goals. I would like to become an academic physician, carrying out research in health-care organization, health-care delivery, or medical devices, in addition to maintaining an active clinical practice. Further on in my career, I would hope to take more of a leadership role in managing a hospital or working in the Public Health Service or similar organization.

Yale is a great place to start on the path to achieving all these aims. The interdisciplinary environment of the university is the perfect place to investigate medical devices and health-care organizations. In terms of management, Yale's MBA program can provide me sound training for any leadership roles in the medical community. Finally, Yale's modern curriculum that emphasizes collaborative learning, patient contact, and clinical skills will provide an excellent background for any future clinician.

In terms of what I can bring to the table, my experiences are quite eclectic. As an aerospace-engineering major, I have been trained to design and build must-not-fail human-mechanical systems. As a volunteer collegiate EMT, I have taken care of a large variety of patients and have taken on a teaching role with my fellow EMTs. Finally, as a student leader, I am familiar with the challenges of running organizations. This background allows me to uniquely help the Yale School of Medicine achieve its goal of creating physician leaders.

As an engineer, my job and predilection is to fix things, whether they be machines, organizations, or people's bodies. I would like to contribute to the field of medicine by helping to improve all of the above: developing better medical devices, establishing organizations that deliver better care, and directly taking care of patients. Yale is an extraordinary place that can prepare me to complete all three goals.

One more practice I've picked up that's worked well for me so far—after an interview and in some cases if I haven't heard from a school in a while, I send an activities update:

Dear Admissions Committee of the Columbia University College of Physicians and Surgeons, Here is an update on my activities since submitting the AMCAS application in June.

1) Throughout the summer and for the beginning of the semester, I served as treasurer (one of the seven executive directors) of the MIT Career Fair. On September 21 I oversaw the largest and most profitable career fair in the history of the institute. To provide context, the previous year's fair saw approximately 300 companies and brought in approximately $550,000 in revenue for MIT. This year's fair saw approximately 350 companies and brought in over $750,000 of revenue, while our expenses only increased by $40,000 (http://tech.mit.edu/V131/N39/career.html).

2) My research into functional electrical stimulation continues. After working full-time as a researcher throughout the summer, I have cut back to about six hours a week during this semester. I will likely publish a paper at the end of this semester or next, and I will be an author. I have proposed a new direction for the study: working with paraplegic patients at the Lahey Clinic in Burlington, Massachusetts, to acquire baseline data in the absence of conscious sensory response. I am currently seeking a neurologist to partner with at the clinic (several have expressed interest) and will submit a proposal to the IRB soon.

3) As I was working full-time over the summer, I took night classes at Harvard Summer School to fulfill my premedical requirements. I received an A- in Biochemistry with Lab and a B in Molecular Biology with Lab.

4) I was selected as the MIT Undergraduate Association representative to the MIT Medical Consumers Advisory Commission for the 2011–12 academic year. The commission's role is to provide recommendations on how best MIT Medical can meet the needs of the community. At the first meeting, I introduced a proposal to study the rates of colds and general illnesses among students grouped by residence hall. If any dorms are hot spots of disease, it can be inferred that the dorm harbors particularly unhygienic conditions, and MIT Medical and Facilities can take steps to address the cause. The proposal was taken up for further consideration by the medical director.

5) As an EMT, I have been involved with many incidents involving student mental-health issues. Consequently, after two undergraduate suicides in two months, I arranged a meeting on November 2, 2011, with the dean of student-support services and MIT Medical's clinical director for campus life. I advocated changes to address several shortcomings of the current, relatively opaque system that discourages the reporting of other students' possible suicidal behavior to MIT Mental Health. The dean then took the shortcomings and suggestions to the chancellor, and discussion of possible improvements continues.

6) I also tried my hand at sailing in my nonexistent free time and earned a sailing card at the MIT Sailing Pavilion.

Thank you again for your consideration of me for membership in your class of 2016. I am truly excited by the opportunities and curriculum at P&S.

Questions from My Columbia Interview

1. Before the interview itself, the dean of admissions sat all the applicants interviewing that day around a room and went around asking about an "interesting thing" in each of our applications. For me, it was my service as an EMT. He also asked us to tell everyone about an activity "that brings us bliss."
2. The interview was open-file, and the interviewer had a few specific questions about my research and work as an EMT. The interviewer asked, "Have you considered what specialty to pursue?", and then asked some public-policy questions. Afterwards, we had an extended discussion about various primary-care issues, as the doctor interviewing me was a internal medicine physician.

I highly recommend for interviews that applicants familiarize themselves with medical specialties and current controversies and issues in the various fields. Having been interviewed by a primary-care doctor at Columbia, when she asked about questions I had, I was able to ask, "So, what's your opinion on PSA testing/mammograms?" (When interviewed by an OB/GYN, I could instead bring up the C-section versus forceps versus natural-birth controversy. For a surgeon, I instead brought up palliative care and specialization / scope of practice issues.) My interviews have all gone exceptionally well once my interviewer realizes I know something about his or her specialty.

Two great books that I've found to be very good at covering current medical issues are *Complications* and *Better*, both by Atul Gawande. His blog is quite informative, too (his recent article about coaching in surgery and another about palliative-care failures were both extraordinarily informative). I always tell my premed underclassmen friends to read them.

Comment: Never mention the weather or activities—you're going to medical school, not selecting a vacation spot. This student did an excellent job of researching each school he was applying to.

RESOURCES

ABOUT.COM: THE *NEW YORK TIMES* NEWS SERVICE AND SYNDICATE

"Many Students Have the Grades and the MCAT Scores—How Will You Stand Out?" by Andrea Santiago, About.com, December 12, 2011.

ASSOCIATION OF AMERICAN MEDICAL COLLEGES

Average MCAT Scores and GPAs for Applicants and Matriculants: Applicant Matriculation File as of October 19, 2010

US Medical School First-Time Applicants, 2001–2011: AAMC Data Warehouse Applicant Matriculation File

US Medical School Total Applicants, 2001–2011: AAMC Data Warehouse Applicant Matriculation File

Applicants to US Medical Schools, 2004–2011: AAMC Data Warehouse Applicant Matriculation File

US Medical School First-Year Enrollment, 2001–2011: AAMC Data Warehouse Applicant Matriculation File

First-Year Enrollees to US Medical Schools, 2004–2011: AAMC Data Warehouse Applicant Matriculation File

US Medical School First-Time Applicants by Gender, 2001–2011: AAMC Data Warehouse Applicant Matriculation File

US Medical School First-Year Enrollees by Gender, 2001–2011: AAMC Data Warehouse Applicant Matriculation File

First-Year Enrollees and Total Applicants to US Medical Schools by Gender, 2011: AAMC Data Warehouse Applicant Matriculation File

US Medical School Applicants and Students 1982–1983 to 2010–2011 Charts

Residency Applicants of US Medical Schools by Specialty and Sex, 2010

Getting into Medical School: www.aamc.org

Exploring a Medical Career: www.aamc.org

Creating a Study Plan: www.aamc.org

Candidates: www.aamc.org

The 2012 MCAT Essentials

The Road to Becoming a Doctor

"Identifying Behaviors of Successful Medical Students and Residents": November 2001, vol. 1, no. 4

MODERN HEALTH CARE

"Medical School Applications Hit New Record, Enrollment up 3%, AAMC Finds," by Ashok Selvam, *Modern Healthcare*, October 24, 2011

"New Rounds for Med Students: Revised Admissions Test, Changing Focus for Essential Skills Will Bring a Fresh Look to the Next Generation of Physicians," by Andis Robeznieks, *Modern Healthcare*, February 27, 2012

YALE DAILY NEWS

"Future Pre-Meds Will Take New MCAT," by Traci Tillman, *Yale Daily News*, April 6, 2011

SAMPLE MMI QUESTIONS

https://www.mcgill.ca/caps/files/caps/guide_mmi-stations.pdf

http://my.science.ubc.ca/files/2014/01/Sample-Questions-2013-2014.pdf

ABOUT THE AUTHOR AND RECEIVING COACHING SERVICES

EDWARD M. GOLDBERG

A native of Chicago's South Side, Mr. Goldberg earned a bachelor of science in marketing from Northern Illinois University and a master of science degree in hospital and health services administration from The Ohio State University. He performed his Administrative Residency at Lutheran General Hospital in Park Ridge, Illinois.

Mr. Goldberg had been a hospital administrator for thirty-eight years, initially being appointed as administrator of Coral Gables Hospital in Florida when he was twenty-five. From 1994 until his retirement in November of 2012, he served as the president/CEO of Saint Alexius Medical Center, a 331-bed medical/surgical facility in Hoffman Estates, Illinois.

Mr. Goldberg had also previously served as a vice president for Columbia/HCA; administrator at Hartgrove Hospital, Chicago, Illinois; administrator at Charter Barclay Hospital, Chicago, Illinois; and regional director with Charter Medical Corporation.

Under his leadership, each hospital Mr. Goldberg was responsible for had significant increases in admissions and outpatient visits. With a strong focus on physician, employee, and patient relations, he consistently achieved some of the nation's highest physician, employee, and patient satisfaction scores. Mr. Goldberg was inducted into the Studer Fire Starter Health Care Hall of Fame in Nashville, Tennessee, on October 10, 2012.

Although this is an updated edition of Mr. Goldberg's first book as an author, he has edited and published an article on cultural sensitivity and has provided numerous presentations to health-care and other organizations on servant leadership, relationship development, and health-care marketing.

Mr. Goldberg is now a coach for individuals applying to medical school, medical-school residencies, dental school, veterinary school, physician assistant, and nurse-practitioner programs. He is available to review personal statements and secondaries and help applicants develop their responses to interview questions via telephone, e-mail, FaceTime, or in person. For pricing and additional information regarding individual coaching, please contact Mr. Goldberg at edward-goldberg@ymail.com.

Mr. Goldberg is married to Linda Trytek and has two grown daughters, Katie and Erica.